Ta[ble of Contents]

Witch's Night Out Quilt

Pumpkin Patch Tablerunner

Witch's Night Out Quilt
Fabric Requirements

Our Witch's Night Out Quilt features the All Hallow's Eve collection by Fig Tree Quilts for Moda Fabrics.

20350-11
Blocks
Fat Quarter

20350-13
Blocks
Fat Quarter

20350-15
Blocks
Fat Quarter

20350-26
Blocks
⅜ yard

20351-15
Blocks
Fat Quarter

20352-11
Blocks
⅜ yard

20352-15
Blocks
Fat Quarter

20352-16
Blocks
Fat Quarter

20353-11
Blocks
⅝ yard

20353-13
Blocks
Fat Quarter

20353-15
Blocks
Fat Quarter

20354-11
Blocks
⅔ yard

20354-13
Blocks
⅜ yard

20354-15
Blocks
Fat Quarter

20355-11
Blocks
⅜ yard

20355-13
Blocks and
Binding
¾ yard

20355-16
Background
4 yards

20356-15
Blocks
Fat Quarter

9900-162
Blocks
½ yard

20350-11
Backing
4 ¼ yards

Introduction

Calling all Spooksters, Ghouls, and Witches! We love Halloween as a festive night that is all fun, no fright. Our Witch's Night Out quilt is a high-spirited broomstick joy ride through pumpkin patches and other Halloween haunts, and it makes a completely be-witch-ing addition to your Fall décor!

The Witch's Night Out quilt conjures everything a witch cannot go without (minus the eye of newt) – a jaunty hat, a feline familiar, a shadowy bat, a bubbling cauldron, and of course a trusty broomstick! All of these blocks are easily pieced, so no curses needed. A variety of seven pieced pumpkin blocks complete this spellbinding scene, and they are found in both the quilt and the bonus Pumpkin Patch Tablerunner for a devilishly darling duo.

Our quilt and tablerunner are made with the All Hallow's Eve fabric collection by Fig Tree Quilts for Moda Fabrics. Feel free to use the same, or use our handy fabric requirements guide on the opposite page to brew up your own combination of fabric. Now, get ready to perform some amazing "stitch-craft"!

Make your home playfully spooky by using individual blocks for pillows, small table toppers or treat bags!

Chevron Pumpkin Block

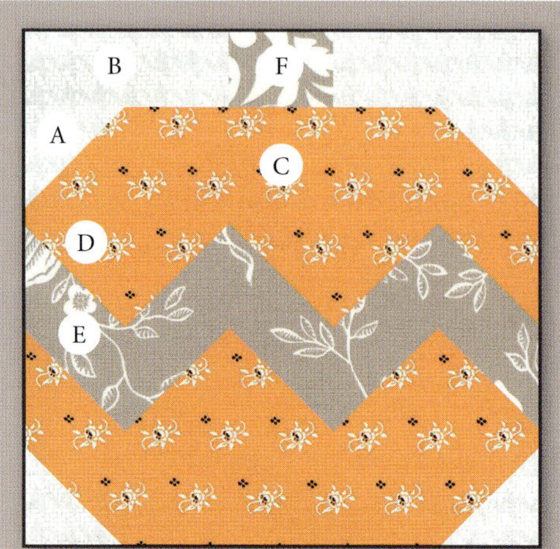

Unfinished size: 5 ½" square
Make four

Cutting Instructions

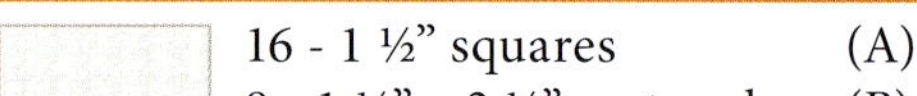

Background (SKU# 20355-16)

	16 - 1 ½" squares	(A)
	8 - 1 ¼" x 2 ½" rectangles	(B)

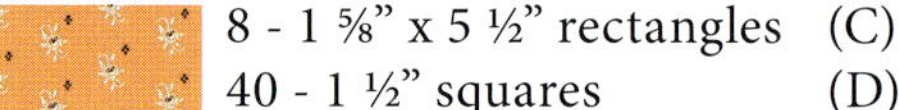

Print Pumpkin (SKU# 20352-11)

	8 - 1 ⅝" x 5 ½" rectangles	(C)
	40 - 1 ½" squares	(D)

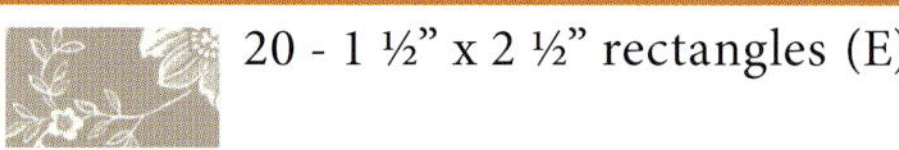

Chevron (SKU# 20350-15)

	20 - 1 ½" x 2 ½" rectangles	(E)

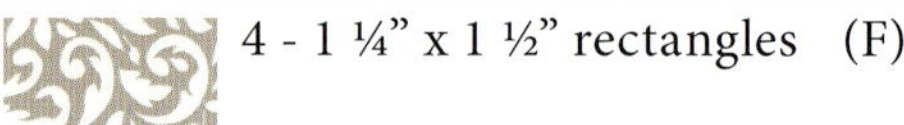

Pumpkin Stem (SKU# 20351-15)

	4 - 1 ¼" x 1 ½" rectangles	(F)

Piecing Instructions

Draw a diagonal line on the wrong side of the Fabric D squares.

With right sides facing, layer a Fabric D square on the top end of a Fabric E rectangle.

Stitch on the drawn line and trim ¼" away from the seam.

 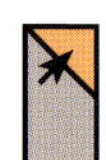

Repeat on the bottom end.

Chevron One Unit should measure 1 ½" x 2 ½".

 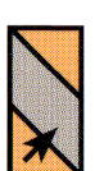

Make twelve.

With right sides facing, layer a Fabric D square on the top end of a Fabric E rectangle.

Stitch on the drawn line and trim ¼" away from the seam.

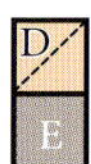 

Repeat on the bottom end.

Chevron Two Unit should measure 1 ½" x 2 ½".

Make eight.

Assemble Unit.

Partial Pumpkin Unit should measure 4 ¾" x 5 ½".

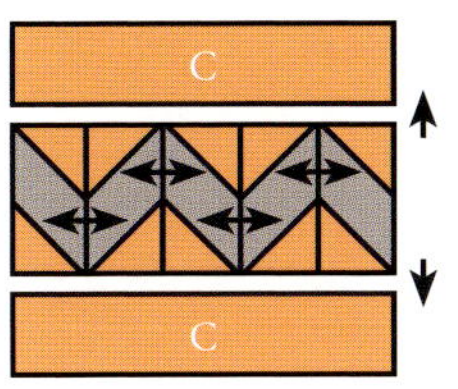 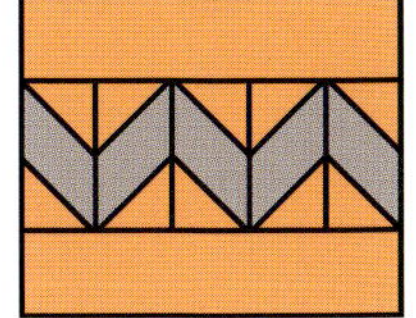

Make four.

Draw a diagonal line on the wrong side of the Fabric A squares.

With right sides facing, layer a Fabric A square on one corner of a Partial Pumpkin Unit.

Stitch on the drawn line and trim ¼" away from the seam.

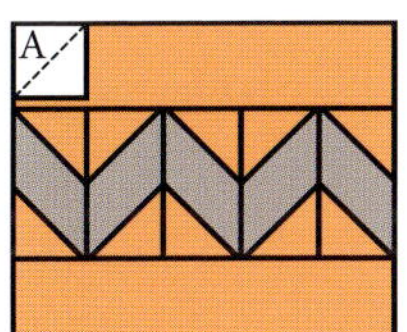 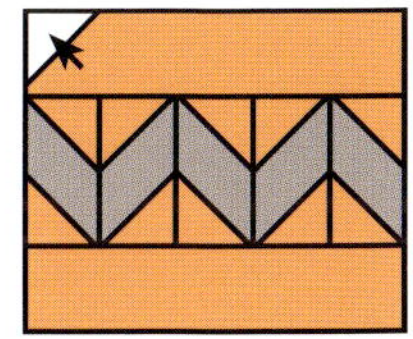

Repeat on the remaining corners.

Pumpkin Unit should measure 4 ¾" x 5 ½".

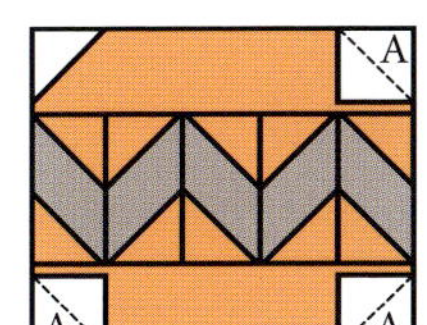 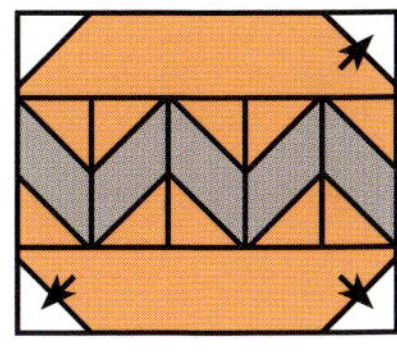

Make four.

Assemble Block.

Chevron Pumpkin Block should measure 5 ½" x 5 ½".

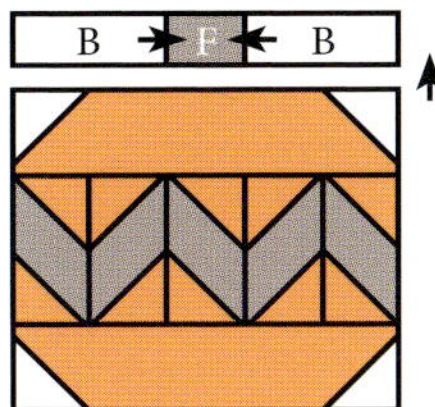 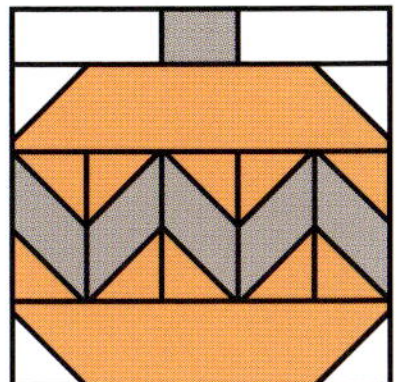

Make four.

Flying Geese Pumpkin Block

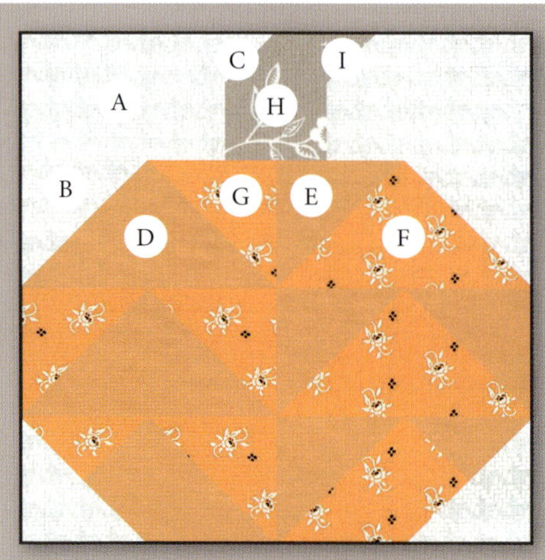

Unfinished size: 5 ½" square
Make four

Cutting Instructions

Background (SKU# 20355-16)

8 - 1 ¾" x 2 ½" rectangles	(A)
16 - 1 ¾" squares	(B)
4 - 1" squares	(C)

Solid Pumpkin (SKU# 9900-162)

12 - 1 ¾" x 3" rectangles	(D)
20 - 1 ¾" squares	(E)

Print Pumpkin (SKU# 20352-11)

12 - 1 ¾" x 3" rectangles	(F)
20 - 1 ¾" squares	(G)

Pumpkin Stem (SKU# 20350-15)

4 - 1 ½" x 1 ¾" rectangles	(H)
4 - 1" squares	(I)

Piecing Instructions

Draw a diagonal line on the wrong side of the Fabric B squares and Fabric G squares.

With right sides facing, layer a Fabric B square on the left end of a Fabric D rectangle.

Stitch on the drawn line and trim ¼" away from the seam.

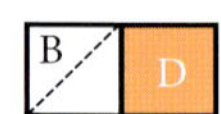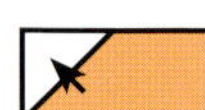

Repeat on the right end with a Fabric G square.

Top Left Pumpkin Unit should measure 1 ¾" x 3".

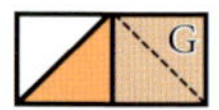

Make four.

Draw a diagonal line on the wrong side of the Fabric E squares.

With right sides facing, layer a Fabric E square on the left end of a Fabric F rectangle.

Stitch on the drawn line and trim ¼" away from the seam.

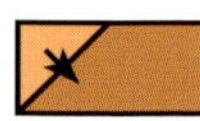

Repeat on the right end with a Fabric B square.

Top Right Pumpkin Unit should measure 1 ¾" x 3".

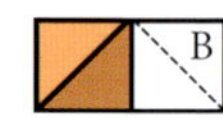

Make four.

Flying Geese Pumpkin Block

With right sides facing, layer a Fabric G square on one end of a Fabric D rectangle.

Stitch on the drawn line and trim ¼" away from the seam.

Repeat on the opposite end.

Left Pumpkin Unit should measure 1 ¾" x 3".

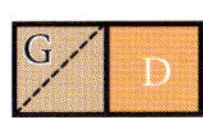

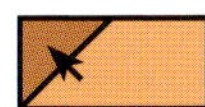

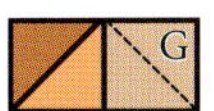

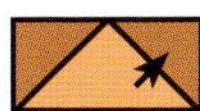

Make eight.

With right sides facing, layer a Fabric E square on one end of a Fabric F rectangle.

Stitch on the drawn line and trim ¼" away from the seam.

Repeat on the opposite end.

Right Pumpkin Unit should measure 1 ¾" x 3".

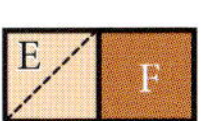

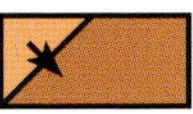

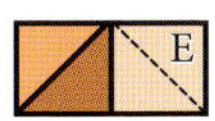

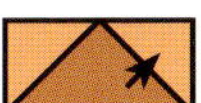

Make eight.

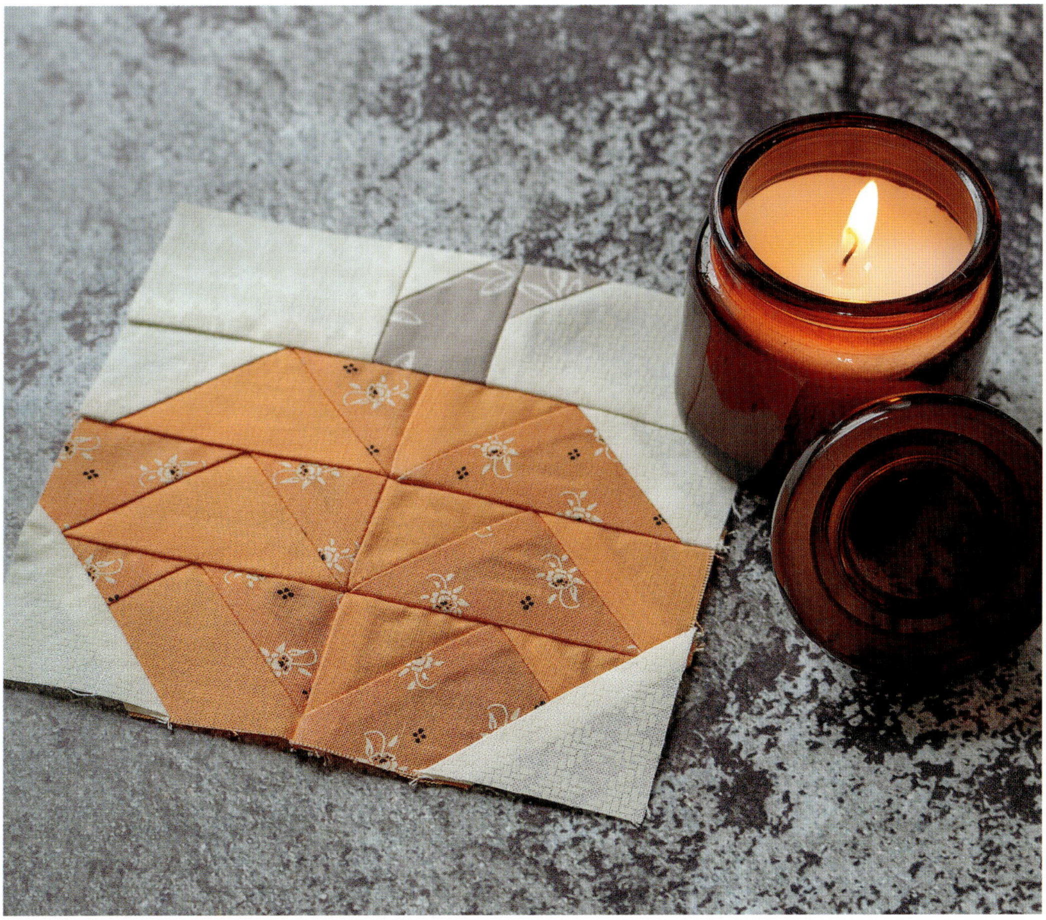

Flying Geese Pumpkin Block

Draw a diagonal line on the wrong side of the Fabric C squares.

With right sides facing, layer a Fabric C square on the top left corner of a Fabric H rectangle.

Stitch on the drawn line and trim ¼" away from the seam.

Left Stem Unit should measure 1 ½" x 1 ¾".

Make four.

Draw a diagonal line on the wrong side of the Fabric I squares.

With right sides facing, layer a Fabric I square on the top left corner of a Fabric A rectangle.

Stitch on the drawn line and trim ¼" away from the seam.

Right Stem Unit should measure 1 ¾" x 2 ½".

Make four.

Assemble Unit.

Pumpkin Unit should measure 5 ½" x 5 ½".

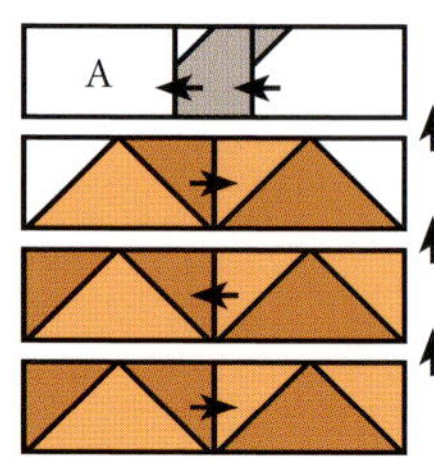 

Make four.

With right sides facing, layer a Fabric B square on the bottom left corner of a Pumpkin Unit.

Stitch on the drawn line and trim ¼" away from the seam.

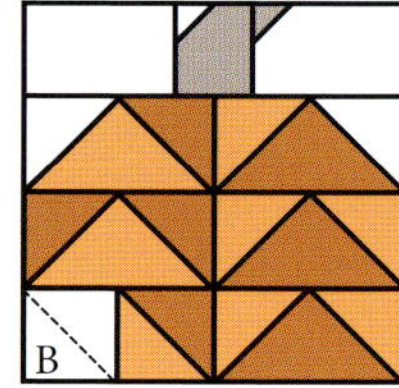 

Repeat on the bottom right corner.

Flying Geese Pumpkin Block should measure 5 ½" x 5 ½".

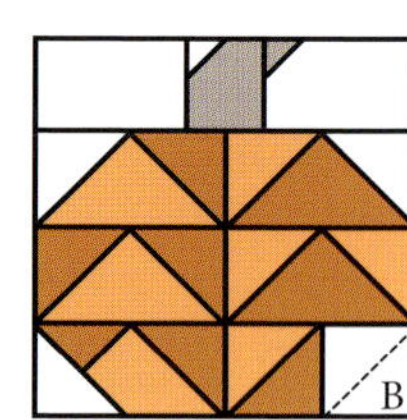 

Make four.

Striped Pumpkin Block

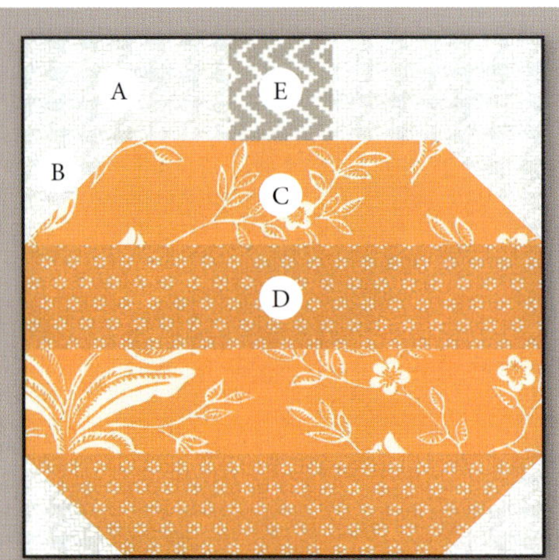

Unfinished size: 5 ½" square
Make four

Cutting Instructions

Background (SKU# 20355-16)

	8 - 1 ½" x 2 ½" rectangles	(A)
	16 - 1 ½" squares	(B)

Print Pumpkin One (SKU# 20350-11)

	8 - 1 ½" x 5 ½" rectangles	(C)

Print Pumpkin Two (SKU# 20354-11)

	8 - 1 ½" x 5 ½" rectangles	(D)

Pumpkin Stem (SKU# 20353-15)

	4 - 1 ½" squares	(E)

Piecing Instructions

Assemble Unit.

Partial Pumpkin Unit should measure 4 ½" x 5 ½".

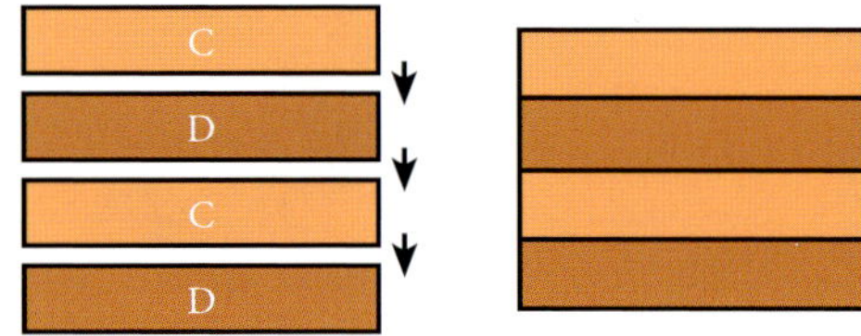

Make four.

Draw a diagonal line on the wrong side of the Fabric B squares.

With right sides facing, layer a Fabric B square on one corner of a Partial Pumpkin Unit.

Stitch on the drawn line and trim ¼" away from the seam.

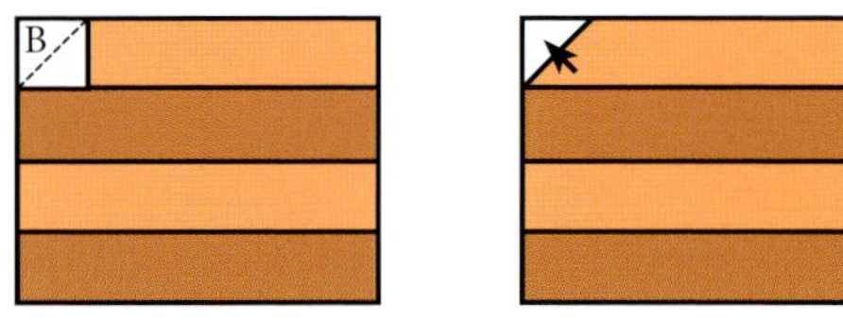

Repeat on the remaining corners.

Pumpkin Unit should measure 4 ½" x 5 ½".

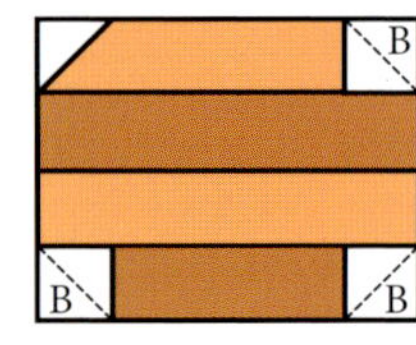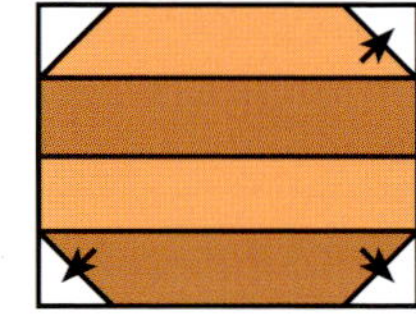

Make four.

Striped Pumpkin Block

Assemble Block.

Striped Pumpkin Block should measure 5 ½" x 5 ½".

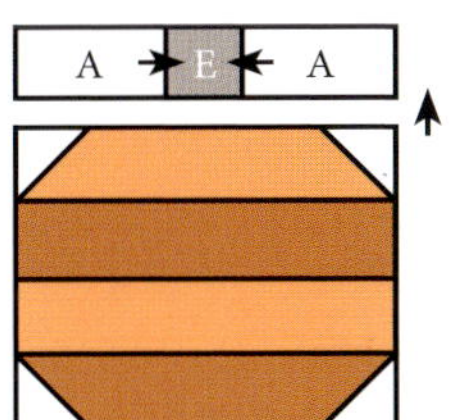 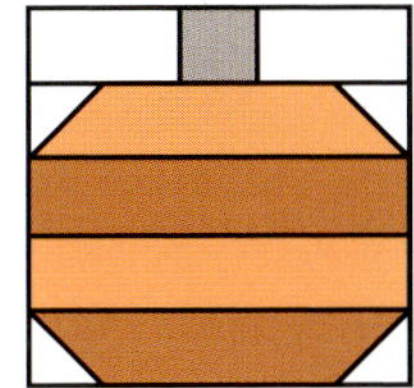

Make four.

Starlight Pumpkin Block

Unfinished size: 8" x 9 ½"
Make three

Cutting Instructions

Background (SKU# 20355-16)

6 - 2" x 4 ¼" rectangles	(A)
12 - 2" squares	(B)
3 - 1 ½" squares	(C)

Pumpkin (SKU# 20354-11)

27 - 2 ½" squares	(D)
18 - 2" x 2 ½" rectangles	(E)

Star Points (SKU# 20350-26)

72 - 1 ½" squares	(F)

Pumpkin Stem (SKU# 20352-15)

3 - 2" squares	(G)
3 - 1 ¼" squares	(H)

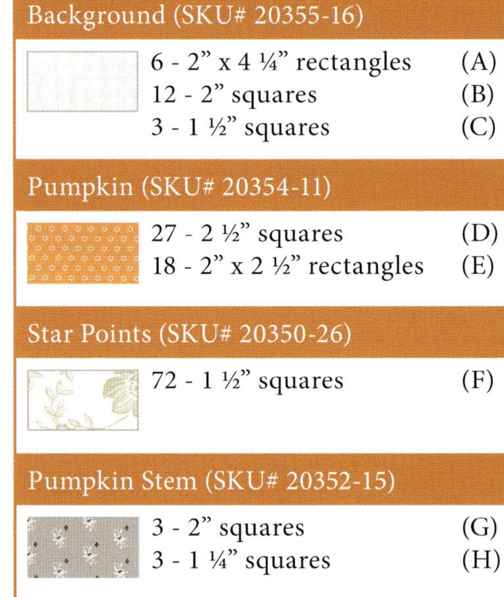

Piecing Instructions

Draw a diagonal line on the wrong side of the Fabric H squares.

With right sides facing, layer a Fabric H square on the top right corner of a Fabric A rectangle.

Stitch on the drawn line and trim ¼" away from the seam.

Left Stem Unit should measure 2" x 4 ¼".

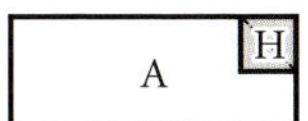 

Make three.

Draw a diagonal line on the wrong side of the Fabric C squares.

With right sides facing, layer a Fabric C square on the top right corner of a Fabric G square.

Stitch on the drawn line and trim ¼" away from the seam.

Right Stem Unit should measure 2" x 2".

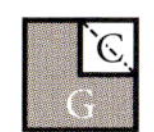 

Make three.

Draw a diagonal line on the wrong side of the Fabric B squares.

With right sides facing, layer a Fabric B square on the top end of a Fabric E rectangle.

Stitch on the drawn line and trim ¼" away from the seam.

Corner One Unit should measure 2" x 2 ½".

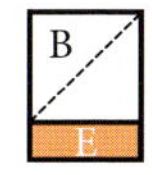 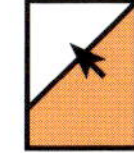

Make six.

With right sides facing, layer a Fabric B square on the bottom end of a Fabric E rectangle.

Stitch on the drawn line and trim ¼" away from the seam.

Corner Two Unit should measure 2" x 2 ½".

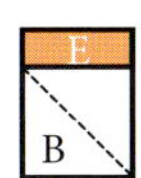 

Make six.

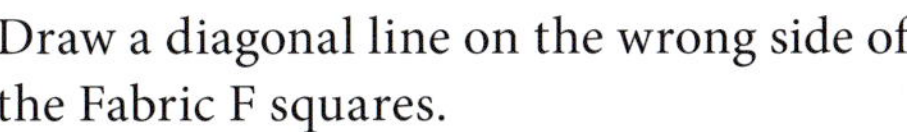

Draw a diagonal line on the wrong side of the Fabric F squares.

With right sides facing, layer a Fabric F square on the bottom left corner of a Fabric D square.

Stitch on the drawn line and trim ¼" away from the seam.

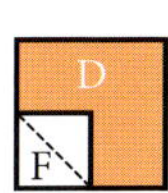 

Repeat on the bottom right corner.

Top and Bottom Star Point Unit should measure 2 ½" x 2 ½".

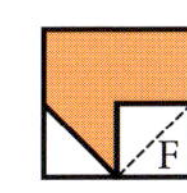 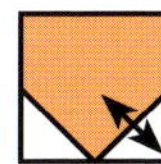

Make twelve.

Starlight Pumpkin Block

With right sides facing, layer a Fabric F square on the top right corner of a Fabric E rectangle.

Stitch on the drawn line and trim ¼" away from the seam.

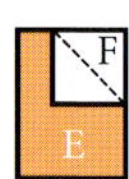 

Repeat on the bottom right corner.

Side Star Point Unit should measure 2" x 2 ½".

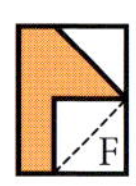 

Make six.

With right sides facing, layer Fabric F squares on the top left and bottom right corners of a Fabric D square.

Stitch on the drawn lines and trim ¼" away from the seam.

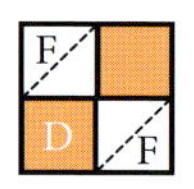 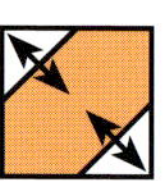

Repeat on the remaining corners.

Center Unit should measure 2 ½" x 2 ½".

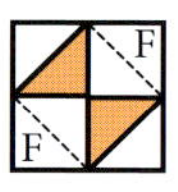 

Make nine.

Starlight Pumpkin Block

Assemble Block.

Starlight Pumpkin Block should measure 8” x 9 ½”.

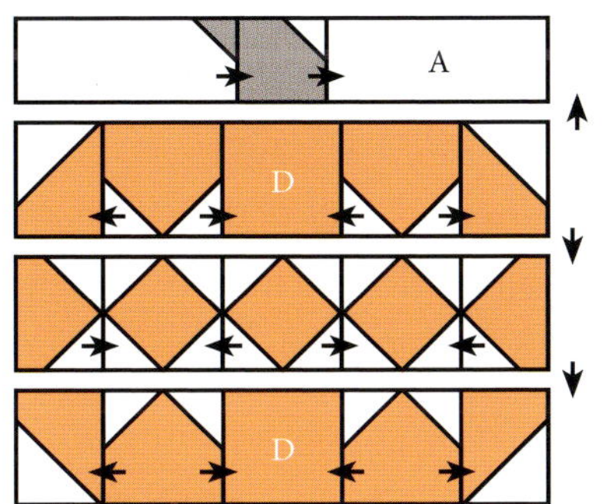

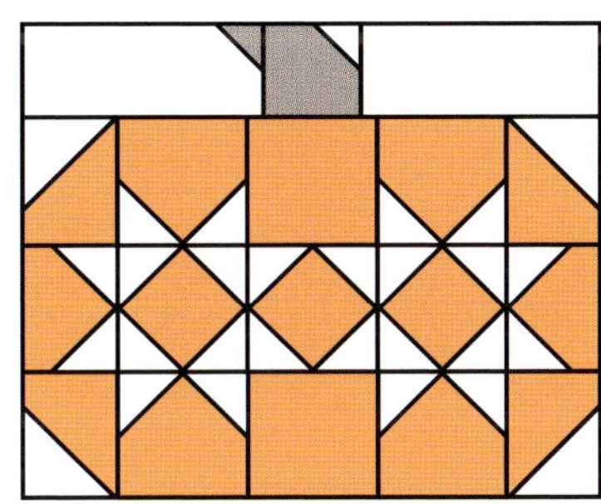

Make three.

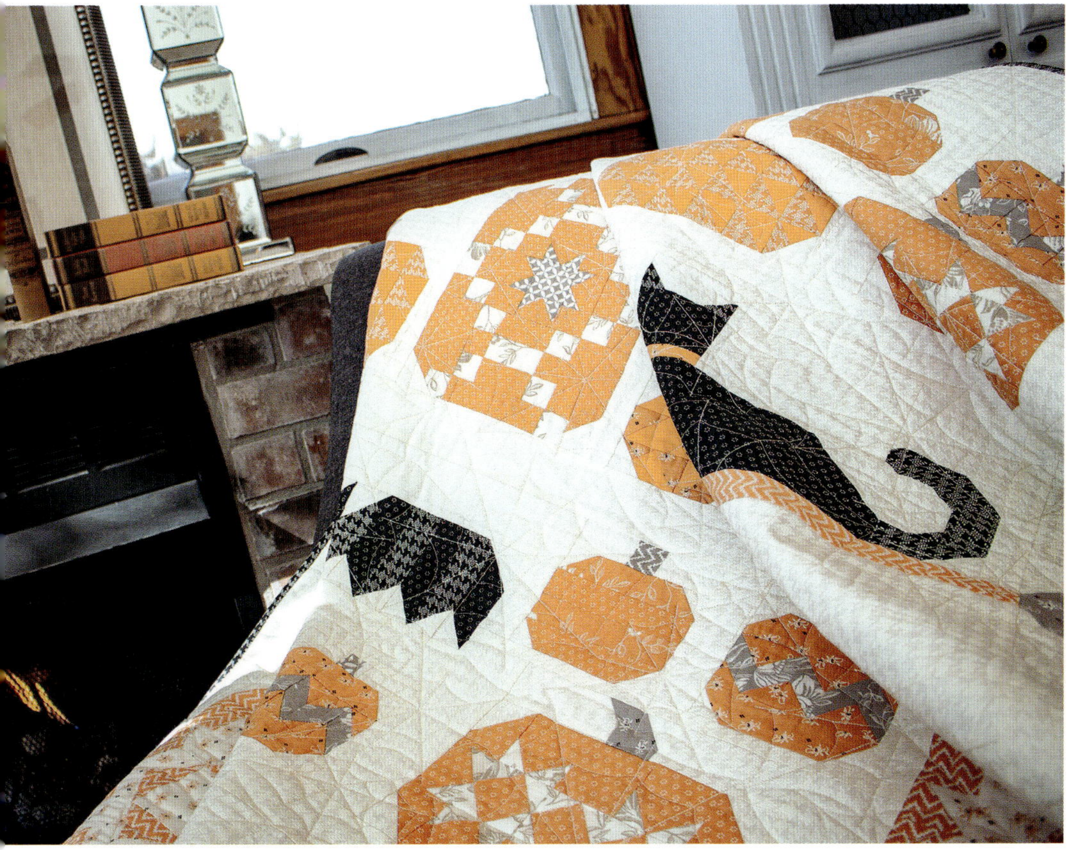

Triangular Pumpkin Block

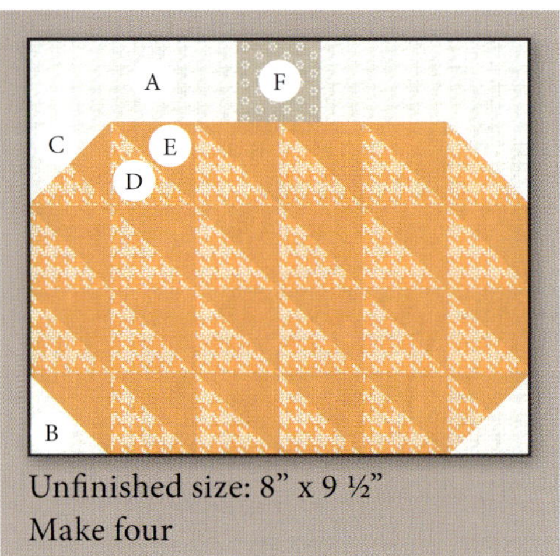

Unfinished size: 8" x 9 ½"
Make four

Cutting Instructions

Background (SKU# 20355-16)

8 - 2" x 4 ¼" rectangles	(A)
4 - 2 ⅜" squares	(B)
8 - 2" squares	(C)

Print Pumpkin (SKU# 20355-11)

46 - 2 ⅜" squares	(D)

Solid Pumpkin (SKU# 9900-162)

46 - 2 ⅜" squares	(E)

Pumpkin Stem (SKU# 20354-15)

4 - 2" squares	(F)

Piecing Instructions

Draw a diagonal line on the wrong side of the Fabric B squares.

With right sides facing, layer a Fabric B square with a Fabric D square.

Stitch ¼" from each side of the drawn line.

Cut apart on the marked line.

Print Half Square Triangle Unit should measure 2" x 2".

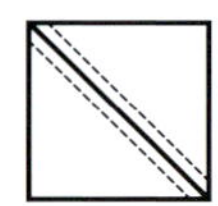 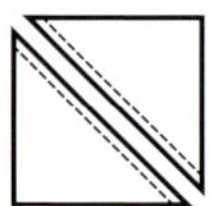 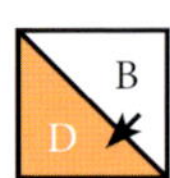

Make four.

With right sides facing, layer a Fabric B square with a Fabric E square.

Stitch ¼" from each side of the drawn line.

Cut apart on the marked line.

Solid Half Square Triangle Unit should measure 2" x 2".

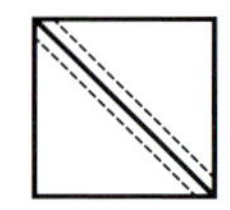  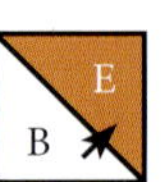

Make four.

Draw a diagonal line on the wrong side of the remaining Fabric D squares.

With right sides facing, layer a marked Fabric D square with a Fabric E square.

Stitch ¼" from each side of the drawn line.

Cut apart on the marked line.

Tonal Half Square Triangle Unit should measure 2" x 2".

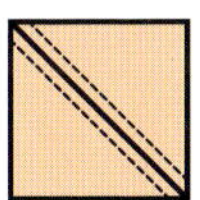 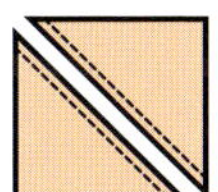 

Make eighty-eight.

Draw a diagonal line on the wrong side of the Fabric C squares.

With right sides facing, layer a Fabric C square with a Tonal Half Square Triangle Unit.

Pay close attention to unit placement.

Stitch on the drawn line and trim ¼" away from the seam.

Top Left Pumpkin Corner Unit should measure 2" x 2".

  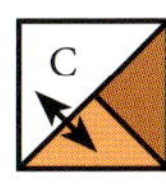

Make four.

With right sides facing, layer a Fabric C square with a Tonal Half Square Triangle Unit.

Pay close attention to unit placement.

Stitch on the drawn line and trim ¼" away from the seam.

Bottom Right Pumpkin Corner Unit should measure 2" x 2".

  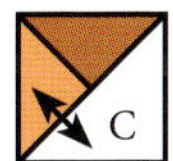

Make four.

Assemble Block.

Triangular Pumpkin Block should measure 8" x 9 ½".

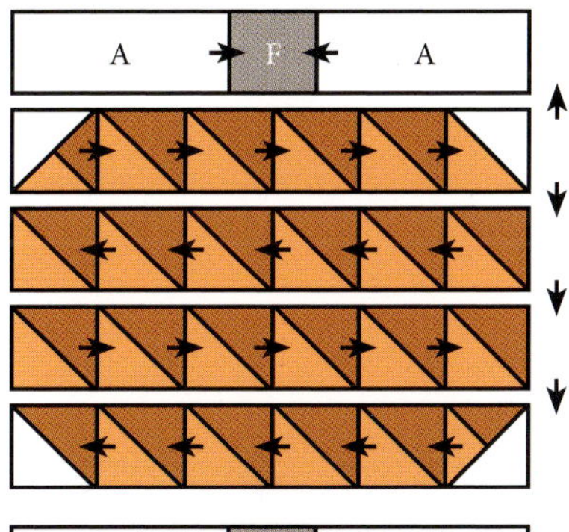

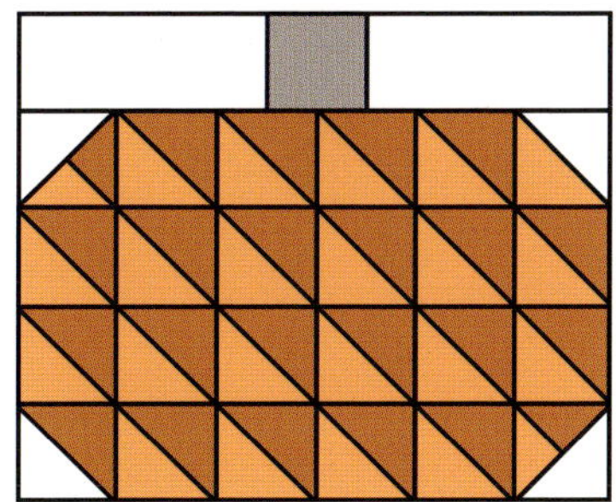

Make four.

Chained Pumpkin Block

Unfinished size: 8 ½" x 13 ½"
Make two

Cutting Instructions

Background (SKU# 20355-16)

	4 - 2" x 4" rectangles	(A)
	8 - 2" squares	(B)

Pumpkin (SKU# 20354-11)

	8 - 2 ½" x 3 ½" rectangles	(C)
	4 - 1 ¾" x 2" rectangles	(D)
	4 - 1 ½" x 4 ½" rectangles	(E)
	8 - 1 ½" x 2 ½" rectangles	(F)
	8 - 1 ½" x 2" rectangles	(G)
	8 - 1 ½" x 1 ¾" rectangles	(H)
	24 - 1 ½" squares	(I)

Chains (SKU# 20350-26)

	4 - 1 ½" x 2 ½" rectangles	(J)
	4 - 1 ½" x 2" rectangles	(K)
	32 - 1 ½" squares	(L)

Star (SKU# 20356-15)

	2 - 2" squares	(M)
	16 - 1 ¼" squares	(N)

Pumpkin Stem (SKU# 20353-15)

	2 - 1 ½" x 2" rectangles	(O)

Piecing Instructions

Draw a diagonal line on the wrong side of the Fabric N squares.

With right sides facing, layer a Fabric N square on the bottom left corner of a Fabric G rectangle.

Stitch on the drawn line and trim ¼" away from the seam.

Repeat on the bottom right corner.

Star Point One Unit should measure 1 ½" x 2".

Make four.

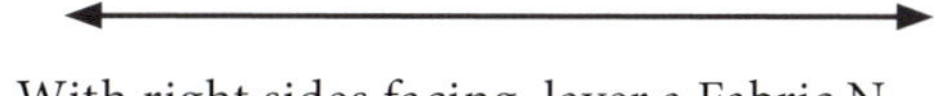

With right sides facing, layer a Fabric N square on the top right corner of a Fabric D rectangle.

Stitch on the drawn line and trim ¼" away from the seam.

Repeat on the bottom right corner.

Star Point Two Unit should measure 1 ¾" x 2".

Make four.

Assemble Unit.

Star Unit should measure 4" x 4 ½".

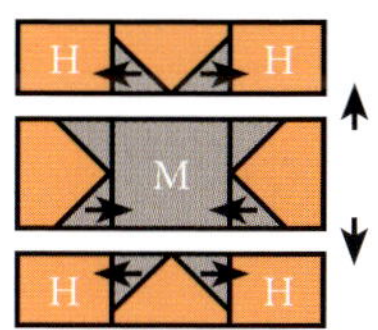 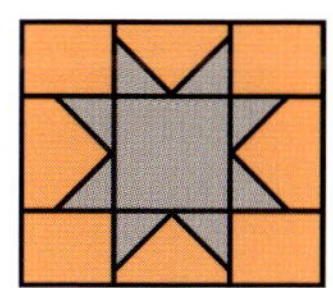

Make two.

Assemble Unit.

Six Patch Pumpkin Unit should measure 2 ½" x 4".

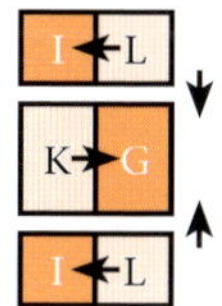 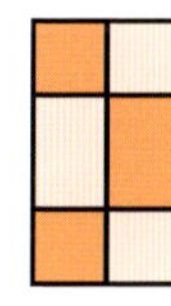

Make four.

Assemble Unit.

Nine Patch Pumpkin Unit should measure 3 ½" x 4 ½".

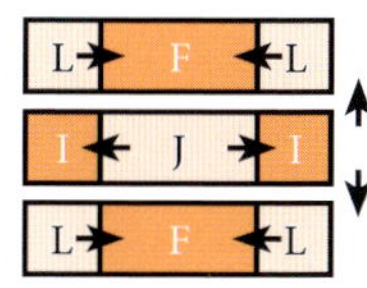 

Make four.

Chained Pumpkin Block

Assemble Unit.

Partial Pumpkin Unit should measure 8 ½" x 12".

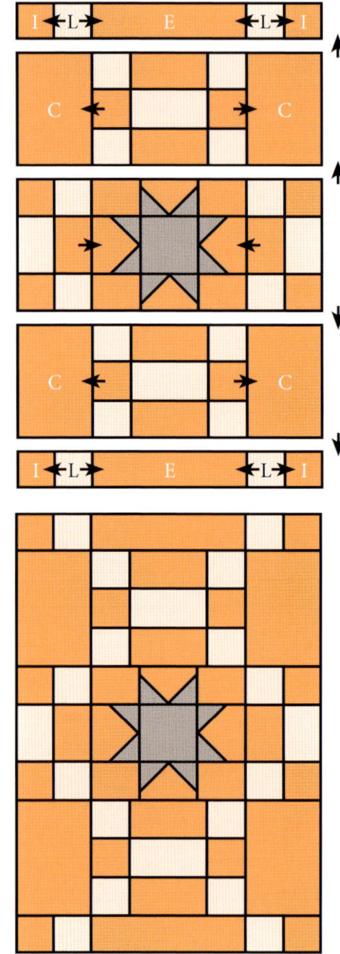

Make two.

Draw a diagonal line on the wrong side of the Fabric B squares.

With right sides facing, layer a Fabric B square on the top left corner of a Partial Pumpkin Unit.

Stitch on the drawn line and trim ¼" away from the seam.

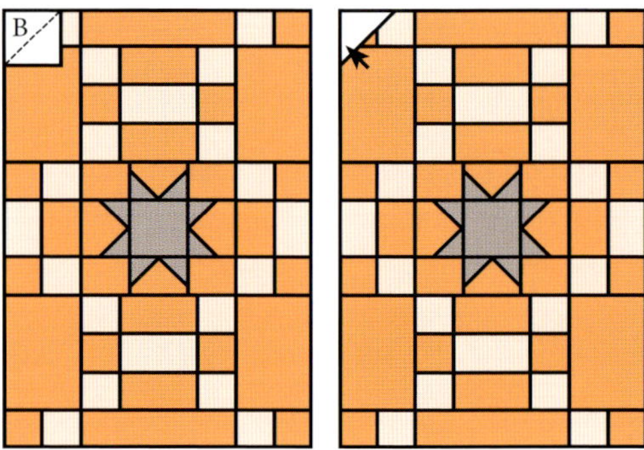

Repeat on the remaining corners.

Pumpkin Unit should measure 8 ½" x 12".

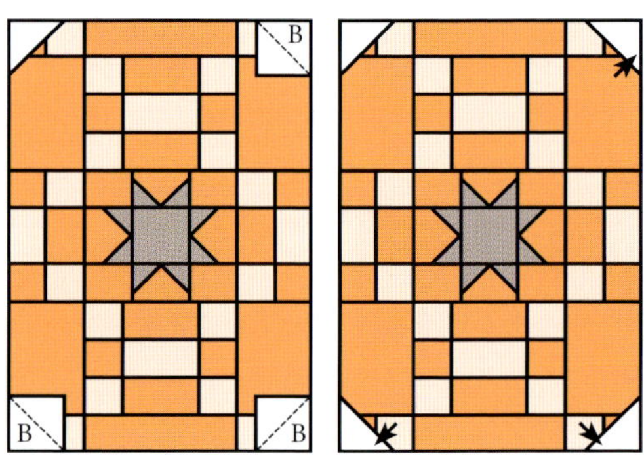

Make two.

Chained Pumpkin Block

Assemble Block.

Chained Pumpkin Block should measure 8 ½" x 13 ½".

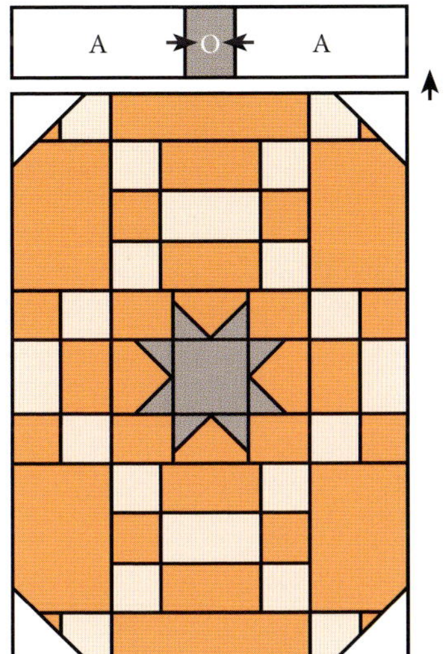

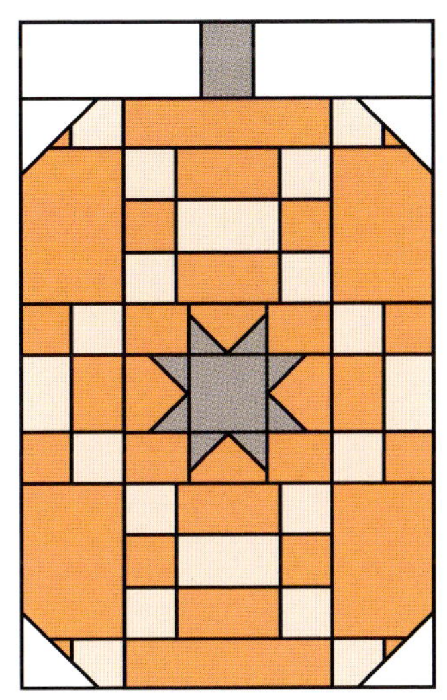

Make two.

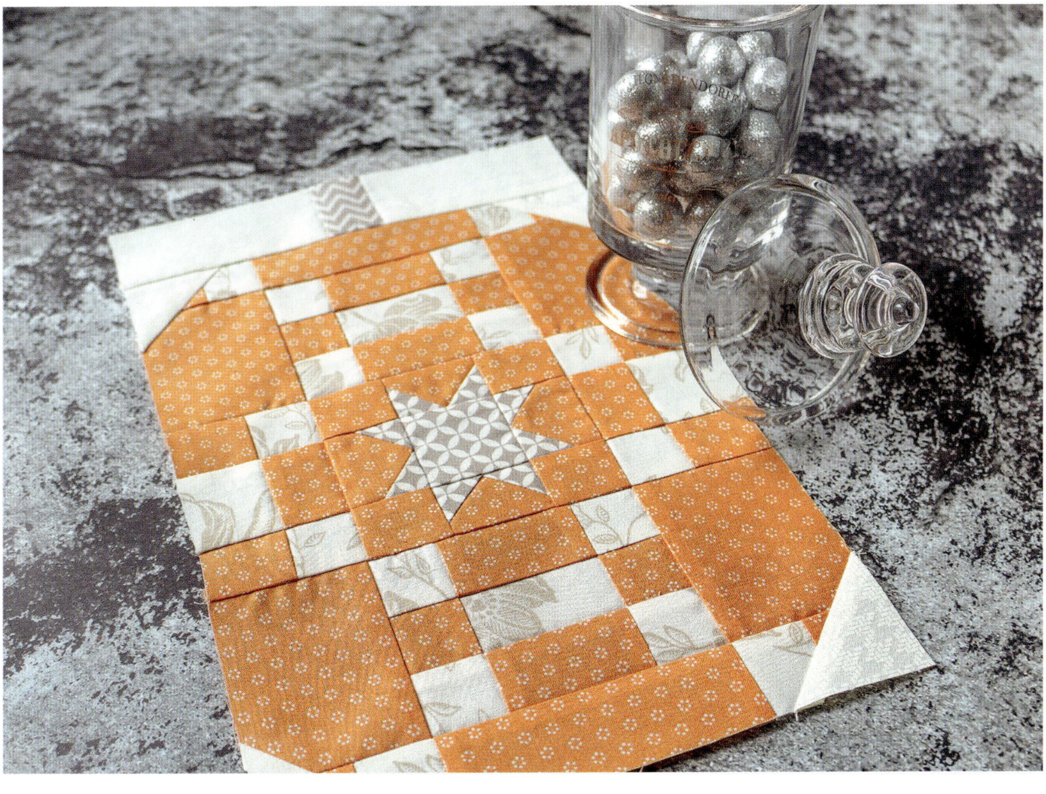

Mosaic Pumpkin Block

Unfinished size: 8 ½" x 13 ½"
Make three

Cutting Instructions

Background (SKU# 20355-16)

	6 - 2" x 4" rectangles	(A)
	12 - 2" squares	(B)

Pumpkin (SKU# 20353-11)

	6 - 2 ½" x 8 ½" rectangles	(C)
	36 - 1 ¾" x 2" rectangles	(D)
	48 - 1 ¾" squares	(E)

Mosaic (SKU# 20352-16)

	3 - 3" squares	(F)
	36 - 1 ¾" x 3" rectangles	(G)
	12 - 1 ¾" squares	(H)

Pumpkin Stem (SKU# 20354-15)

	3 - 1 ½" x 2" rectangles	(I)

Piecing Instructions

Draw a diagonal line on the wrong side of the Fabric B squares.

With right sides facing, layer a Fabric B square on the top left corner of a Fabric C rectangle.

Stitch on the drawn line and trim ¼" away from the seam.

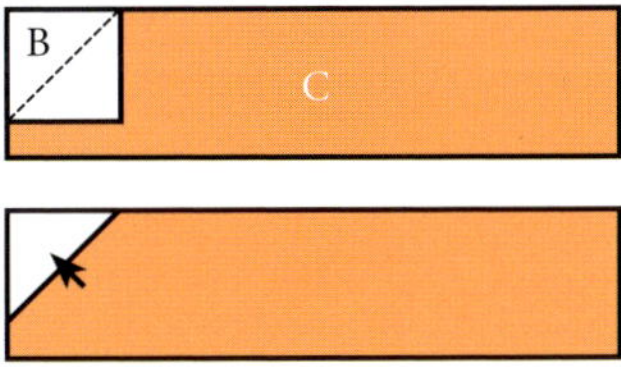

Repeat on the top right corner.

Outer Pumpkin Unit should measure 2 ½" x 8 ½".

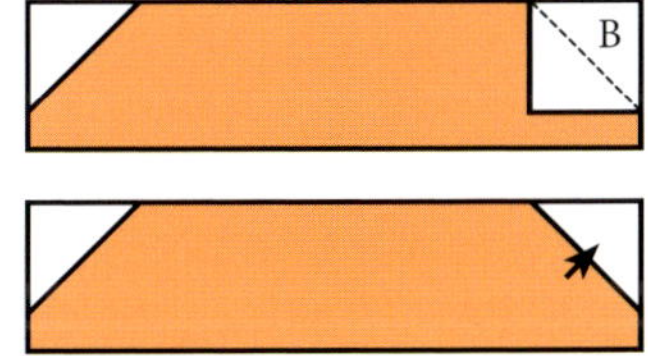

Make six.

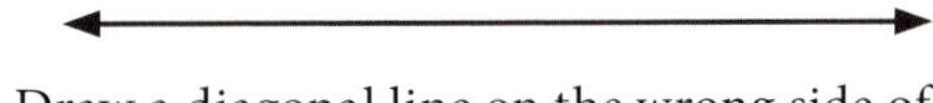

Draw a diagonal line on the wrong side of the Fabric E squares.

With right sides facing, layer a Fabric E square on the top end of a Fabric G rectangle.

Stitch on the drawn line and trim ¼" away from the seam.

Right Corner One Unit should measure 1 ¾" x 3".

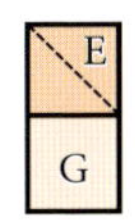

Make six.

Draw a diagonal line on the wrong side of the Fabric H squares.

With right sides facing, layer a Fabric H square on the right end of a Fabric D rectangle.

Stitch on the drawn line and trim ¼" away from the seam.

Left Corner One Unit should measure 1 ¾" x 2".

Make six.

Assemble Unit.

Corner One Unit should measure 3" x 3 ¼".

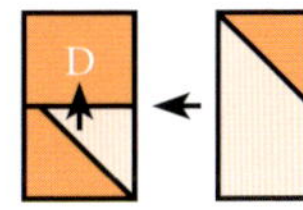

Make six.

With right sides facing, layer a Fabric E square on the top end of a Fabric G rectangle.

Stitch on the drawn line and trim ¼" away from the seam.

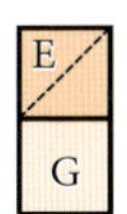

Repeat on the bottom end.

Left Mosaic Point Unit should measure 1 ¾" x 3".

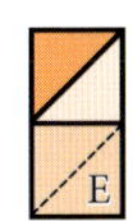

Make six.

Mosaic Pumpkin Block

With right sides facing, layer a Fabric E square on the top end of a Fabric G rectangle.

Stitch on the drawn line and trim ¼" away from the seam.

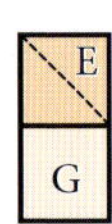 

Repeat on the bottom end.

Right Mosaic Point Unit should measure 1 ¾" x 3".

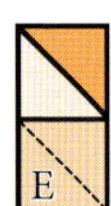 

Make six.

With right sides facing, layer a Fabric E square on the top end of a Fabric G rectangle.

Stitch on the drawn line and trim ¼" away from the seam.

Left Corner Two Unit should measure 1 ¾" x 3".

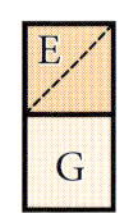 

Make six.

With right sides facing, layer a Fabric H square on the left end of a Fabric D rectangle.

Stitch on the drawn line and trim ¼" away from the seam.

Right Corner Two Unit should measure 1 ¾" x 2".

Make six.

Assemble Unit.

Corner Two Unit should measure 3" x 3 ¼".

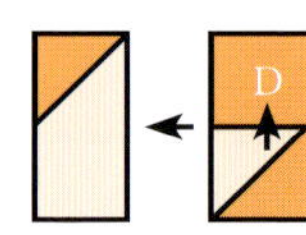 

Make six.

Mark a dot 1 ¾" down from the top left corner on the wrong side of six Fabric D rectangles.

Draw a line from the top right corner to the dot.

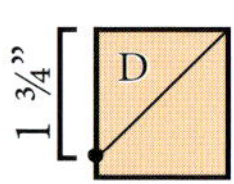

With right sides facing, layer a marked Fabric D rectangle with a Fabric G rectangle.

Stitch on the drawn line and trim ¼" away from the seam.

Partial Top Mosaic Point Unit should measure 1 ¾" x 3 ¼".

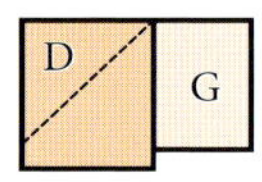 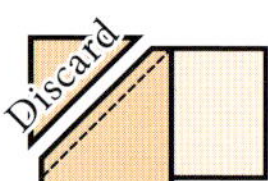 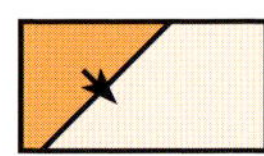

Make six.

With right sides facing, layer a Fabric E square on the right end of a Partial Top Mosaic Point Unit.

Stitch on the drawn line and trim ¼" away from the seam.

Top Mosaic Point Unit should measure 1 ¾" x 3 ¼".

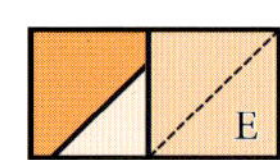 

Make six.

Mosaic Pumpkin Block

Mark a dot 1 ¾" up from the bottom left corner on the wrong side of the remaining Fabric D rectangles.

Draw a line from the bottom right corner to the dot.

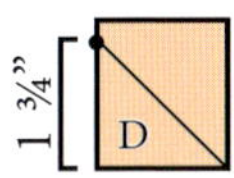

With right sides facing, layer a marked Fabric D rectangle with a Fabric G rectangle.

Stitch on the drawn line and trim ¼" away from the seam.

Partial Bottom Mosaic Point Unit should measure 1 ¾" x 3 ¼".

 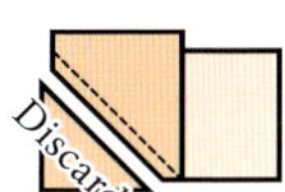 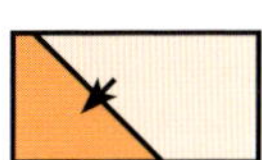

Make six.

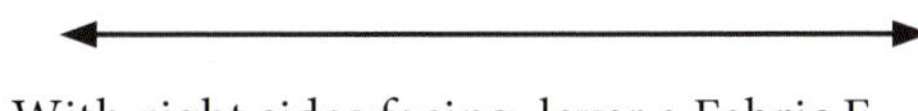

With right sides facing, layer a Fabric E square on the right end of a Partial Bottom Mosaic Point Unit.

Stitch on the drawn line and trim ¼" away from the seam.

Bottom Mosaic Point Unit should measure 1 ¾" x 3 ¼".

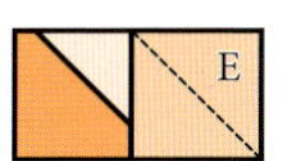 

Make six.

Assemble Unit.

Outer Mosaic Point Unit should measure 3" x 3 ¼".

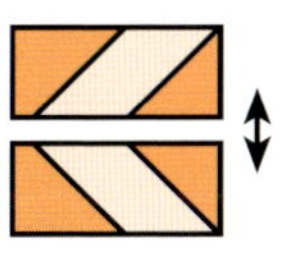 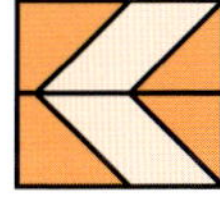

Make six.

Assemble Block.

Mosaic Pumpkin Block should measure 8 ½" x 13 ½".

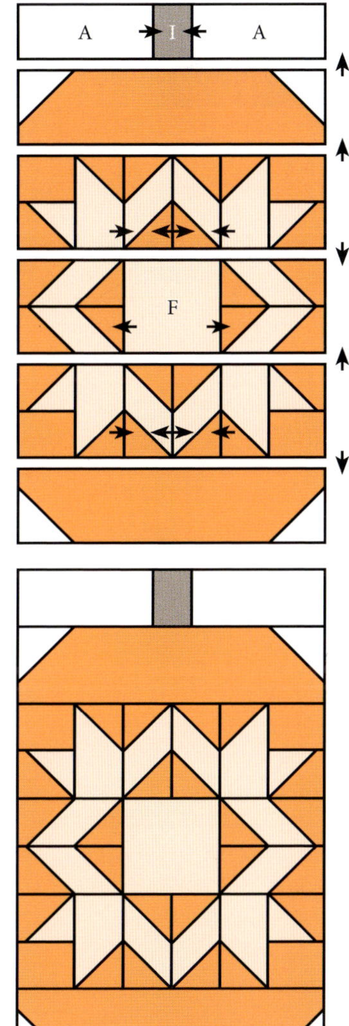

Make three.

Black Cat and Broomstick Block

Unfinished size: 13 ½" x 26 ½"
Make one

Cutting Instructions

Background (SKU# 20355-16)

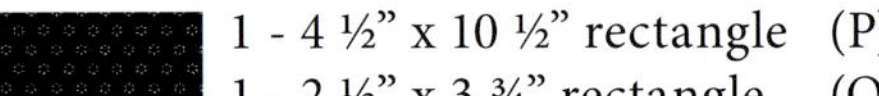

1 - 5 ½" x 11 ½" rectangle	(A)
1 - 4 ½" x 15 ½" rectangle	(B)
1 - 4 ½" x 6 ¾" rectangle	(C)
1 - 3 ¼" x 4" rectangle	(D)
1 - 3 ¼" square	(E)
2 - 2 ½" squares	(F)
1 - 2 ¼" x 3 ¼" rectangle	(G)
1 - 2" x 3 ¾" rectangle	(H)
3 - 2" squares	(I)
2 - 1 ¾" squares	(J)
1 - 1 ½" x 11 ½" rectangle	(K)
2 - 1 ½" x 8 ½" rectangles	(L)
2 - 1 ½" x 2" rectangles	(M)
2 - 1 ½" squares	(N)
2 - ⅞" squares	(O)

Black Cat Head & Body (SKU# 20354-13)

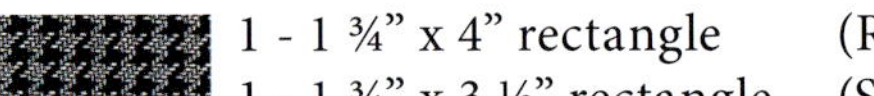

1 - 4 ½" x 10 ½" rectangle	(P)
1 - 2 ½" x 3 ¾" rectangle	(Q)

Black Cat Ears & Tail (SKU# 20355-13)

1 - 1 ¾" x 4" rectangle	(R)
1 - 1 ¾" x 3 ½" rectangle	(S)
1 - 1 ¾" x 3 ¼" rectangle	(T)
2 - 1 ½" squares	(U)
2 - 1 ¼" squares	(V)

Black Cat Collar (SKU# 20352-11)

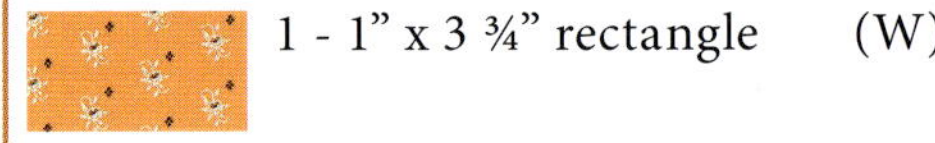

1 - 1" x 3 ¾" rectangle	(W)

Broomstick Handle (SKU# 20353-11)

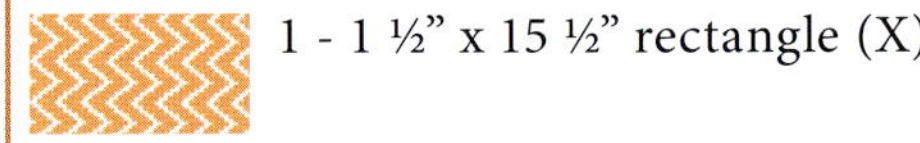

1 - 1 ½" x 15 ½" rectangle	(X)

Broomstick Brush One (SKU# 20352-15)

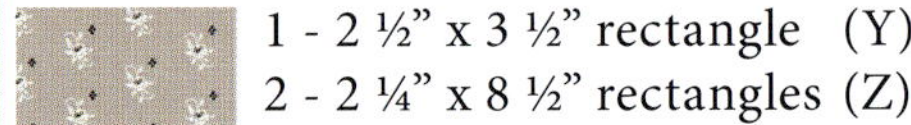

1 - 2 ½" x 3 ½" rectangle	(Y)
2 - 2 ¼" x 8 ½" rectangles	(Z)

Broomstick Brush Two (SKU# 20351-15)

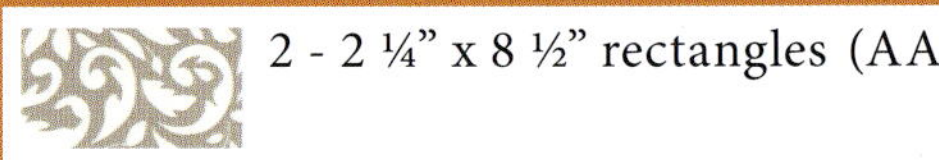

2 - 2 ¼" x 8 ½" rectangles	(AA)

Broomstick Brush Cap (SKU# 20350-11)

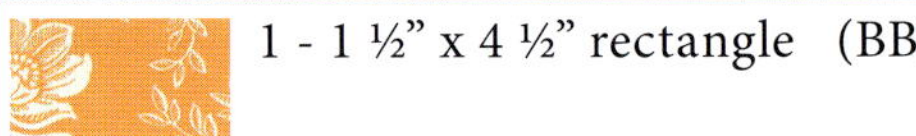

1 - 1 ½" x 4 ½" rectangle	(BB)

Piecing Instructions

Draw a diagonal line on the wrong side of the Fabric U squares.

With right sides facing, layer a Fabric U square on the bottom left corner of the Fabric H rectangle.

Stitch on the drawn line and trim ¼" away from the seam.

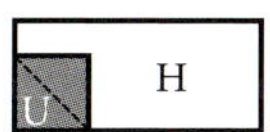 

Repeat on the bottom right corner.

Cat Ears Unit should measure 2" x 3 ¾".

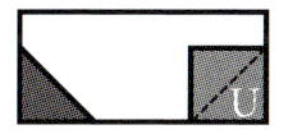 

Make one.

Draw a diagonal line on the wrong side of the Fabric J squares and Fabric O squares.

With right sides facing, layer a Fabric J square on the right end of the Fabric R rectangle.

Stitch on the drawn line and trim ¼" away from the seam.

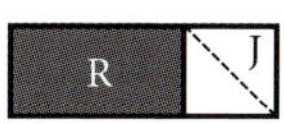 

Repeat on the top and bottom left corners with Fabric O squares.

Top Cat Tail Unit should measure 1 ¾" x 4".

Make one.

Assemble Unit.

Top Cat Unit should measure 4 ½" x 13 ½".

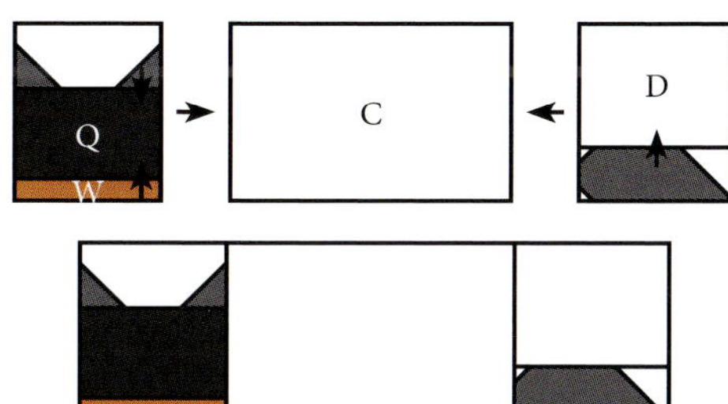

Make one.

Draw a diagonal line on the wrong side of the Fabric V squares.

With right sides facing, layer a Fabric V square on the top right corner of the Fabric G rectangle.

Stitch on the drawn line and trim ¼" away from the seam.

Repeat on the bottom right corner.

Middle Cat Tail Unit should measure 2 ¼" x 3 ¼".

Make one.

Black Cat and Broomstick Block

Assemble Unit.

Partial Bottom Cat Tail Unit should measure 3 ½" x 4 ½".

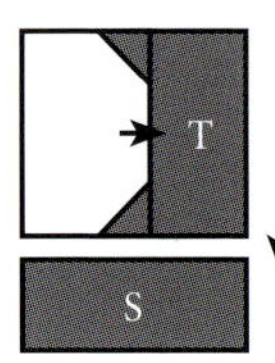 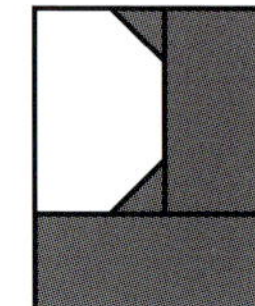

Make one.

Draw a diagonal line on the wrong side of the Fabric I squares.

With right sides facing, layer a Fabric I square on the bottom right corner of the Partial Bottom Cat Tail Unit.

Stitch on the drawn line and trim ¼" away from the seam.

Bottom Cat Tail Unit should measure 3 ½" x 4 ½".

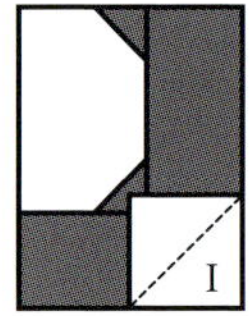 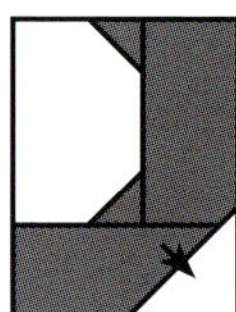

Make one.

Draw a diagonal line on the wrong side of the Fabric E square.

With right sides facing, layer a Fabric J square on the bottom left corner of the Fabric P rectangle.

Stitch on the drawn line and trim ¼" away from the seam.

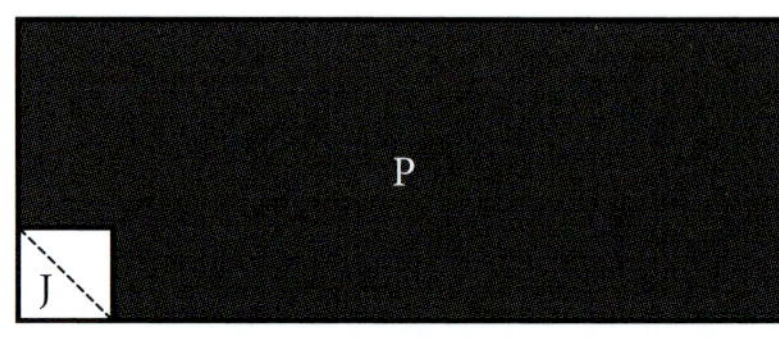

Repeat on the top right corner with the Fabric E square.

Cat Body Unit should measure 4 ½" x 10 ½".

Make one.

Assemble Unit.

Cat Unit should measure 8 ½" x 13 ½".

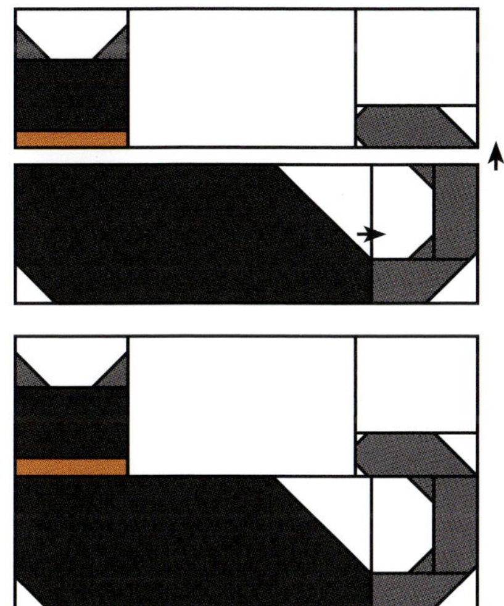

Make one.

Assemble Unit.

Left Black Cat and Broomstick Unit should measure 13 ½" x 15 ½".

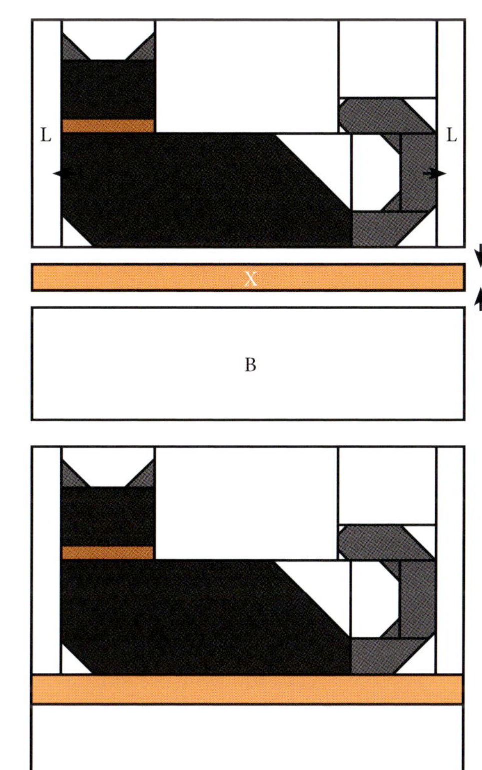

Make one.

Black Cat and Broomstick Block

Draw a diagonal line on the wrong side of the Fabric N squares.

With right sides facing, layer a Fabric N square on the top left corner of the Fabric Y rectangle.

Stitch on the drawn line and trim ¼" away from the seam.

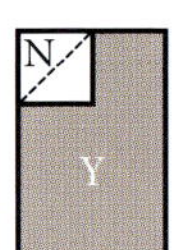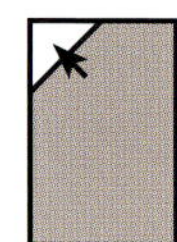

Repeat on the bottom left corner.

Left Broomstick Unit should measure 2 ½" x 3 ½".

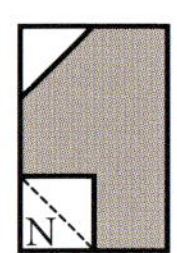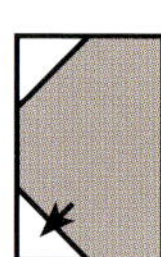

Make one.

With right sides facing, layer a Fabric I square on the top left corner of a Fabric Z rectangle.

Stitch on the drawn line and trim ¼" away from the seam.

Top Broomstick Unit should measure 2 ¼" x 8 ½".

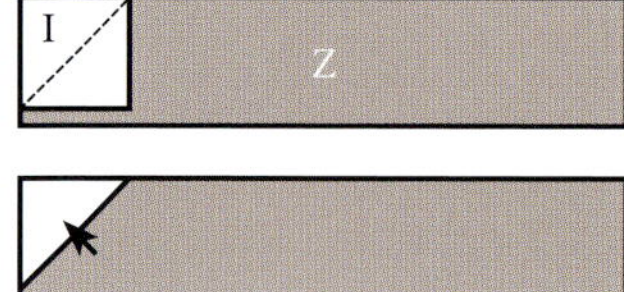

Make one.

With right sides facing, layer a Fabric I square on the bottom left corner of a Fabric AA rectangle.

Stitch on the drawn line and trim ¼" away from the seam.

Bottom Broomstick Unit should measure 2 ¼" x 8 ½".

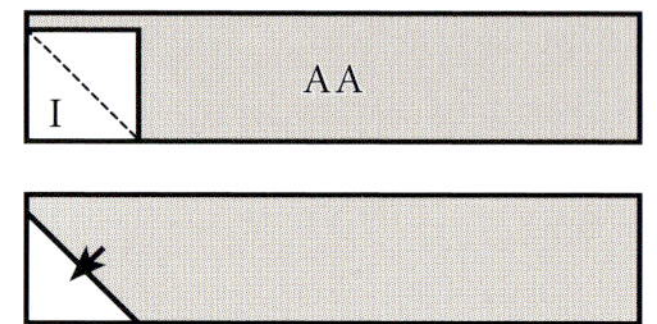

Make one.

Assemble Unit.

Broomstick Unit should measure 7 ½" x 11 ½".

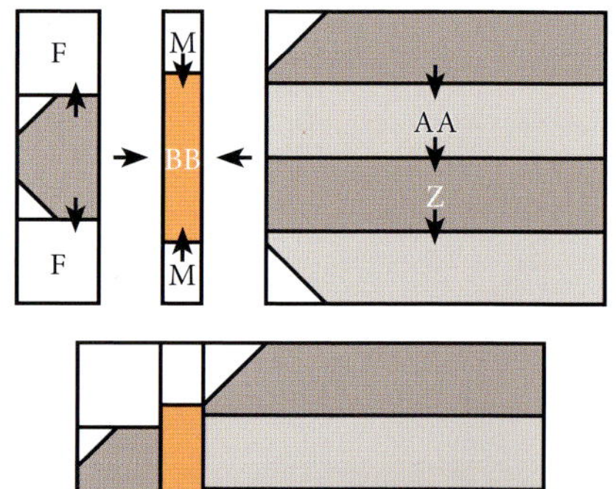

Make one.

Black Cat and Broomstick Block

Assemble Block.

Black Cat and Broomstick Block should measure 13 ½" x 26 ½".

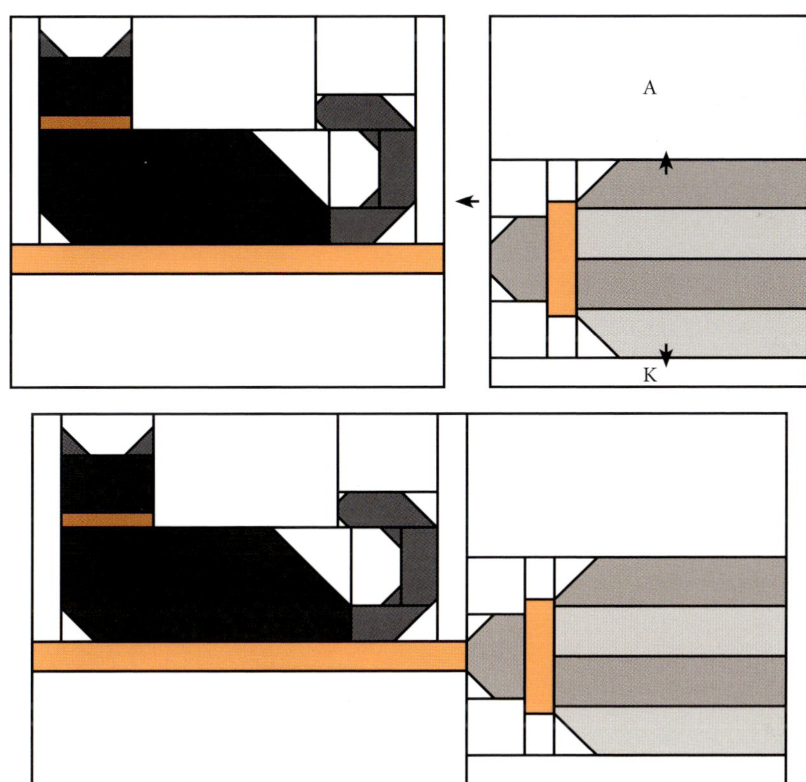

Make one.

Bubbling Cauldron Block

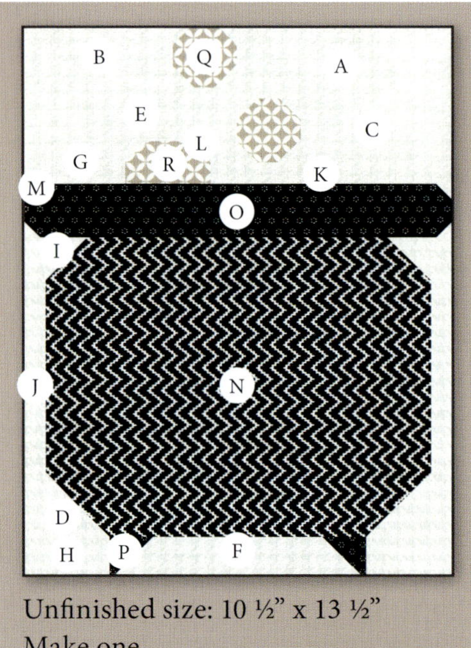

Unfinished size: 10 ½" x 13 ½"
Make one

Cutting Instructions

Background (SKU# 20355-16)

1 - 2 ¼" x 5" rectangle	(A)
1 - 2" x 4 ½" rectangle	(B)
1 - 2" x 3 ½" rectangle	(C)
2 - 2" squares	(D)
1 - 1 ¾" x 6" rectangle	(E)
1 - 1 ½" x 6 ½" rectangle	(F)
1 - 1 ½" x 3" rectangle	(G)
2 - 1 ½" x 2 ½" rectangles	(H)
3 - 1 ½" squares	(I)
2 - 1" x 7 ½" rectangles	(J)
1 - 1" x 5" rectangle	(K)
10 - 1" squares	(L)
4 - ⅞" squares	(M)

Cauldron Pot (SKU# 20353-13)

1 - 7 ½" x 9 ½" rectangle	(N)

Cauldron Rim and Feet (SKU# 20354-13)

1 - 1 ¾" x 10 ½" rectangle	(O)
2 - 1 ½" squares	(P)

Bubbles (SKU# 20356-15)

2 - 2" squares	(Q)
1 - 1 ½" x 2 ½" rectangle	(R)

Piecing Instructions

Draw a diagonal line on the wrong side of the Fabric L squares.

With right sides facing, layer a Fabric L square on one corner of a Fabric Q square.

Stitch on the drawn line and trim ¼" away from the seam.

Repeat on the remaining corners.

Small Bubble Unit should measure 2" x 2".

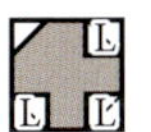 

Make two.

With right sides facing, layer a Fabric L square on the top left corner of the Fabric R rectangle.

Stitch on the drawn line and trim ¼" away from the seam.

Repeat on the top right corner.

Large Bubble Unit should measure 1 ½" x 2 ½".

Make one.

Assemble Unit.

Left Bubbling Unit should measure 4 ¼" x 6".

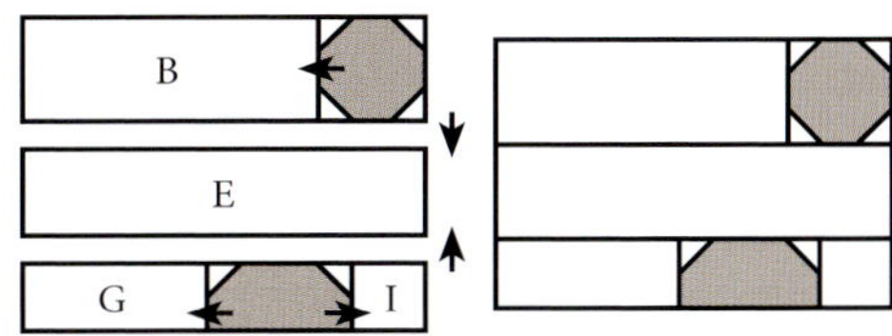

Make one.

Assemble Unit.

Right Bubbling Unit should measure 4 ¼" x 5".

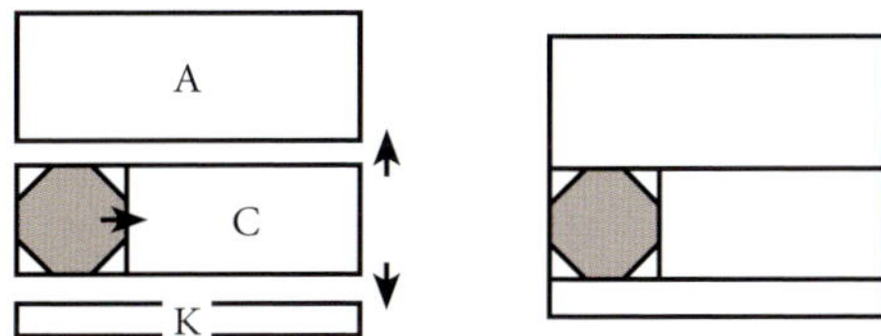

Make one.

Assemble Unit.

Bubbling Unit should measure 4 ¼" x 10 ½".

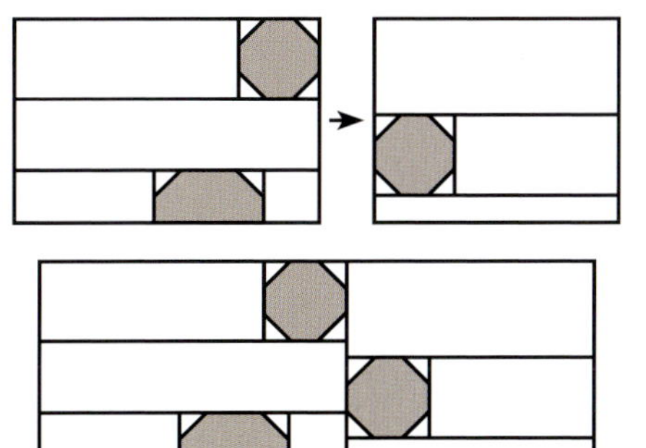

Make one.

Bubbling Cauldron Block

Draw a diagonal line on the wrong side of the Fabric M squares.

With right sides facing, layer a Fabric M square on one corner of the Fabric O rectangle.

Stitch on the drawn line and trim ¼" away from the seam.

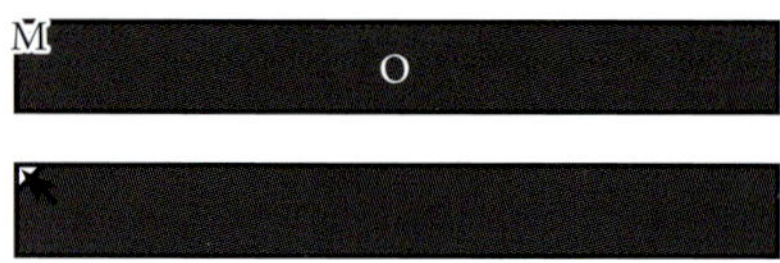

Repeat on the remaining corners.

Cauldron Rim Unit should measure 1 ¾" x 10 ½".

Make one.

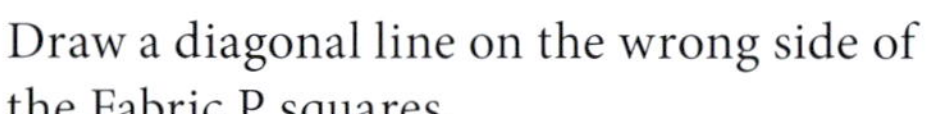

Draw a diagonal line on the wrong side of the Fabric P squares.

With right sides facing, layer a Fabric P square on the left end of the Fabric F rectangle.

Stitch on the drawn line and trim ¼" away from the seam.

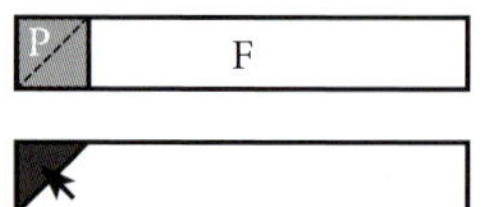

Repeat on the right end.

Cauldron Feet Unit should measure 1 ½" x 6 ½".

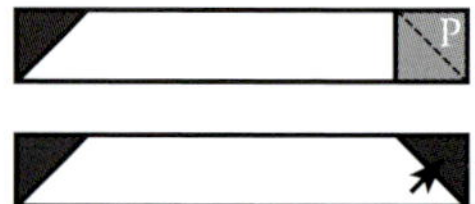

Make one.

Draw a diagonal line on the wrong side of the remaining Fabric I squares and the Fabric D squares.

With right sides facing, layer a marked Fabric I square on the top left corner of the Fabric N rectangle.

Stitch on the drawn line and trim ¼" away from the seam.

Repeat on the top right corner with a Fabric I square and the bottom left and bottom right corners with Fabric D squares.

Cauldron Pot Unit should measure 7 ½" x 9 ½".

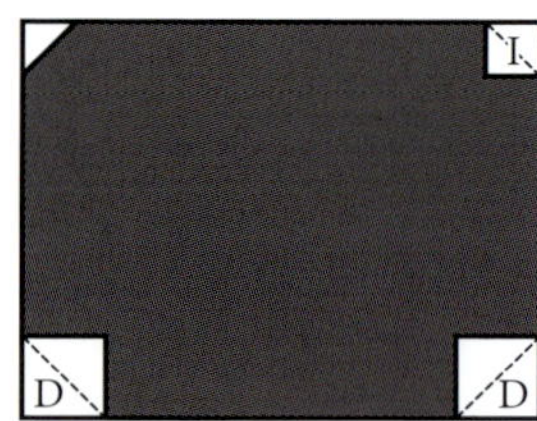

Make one.

Bubbling Cauldron Block

Assemble Block.

Bubbling Cauldron Block should measure 10 ½" x 13 ½".

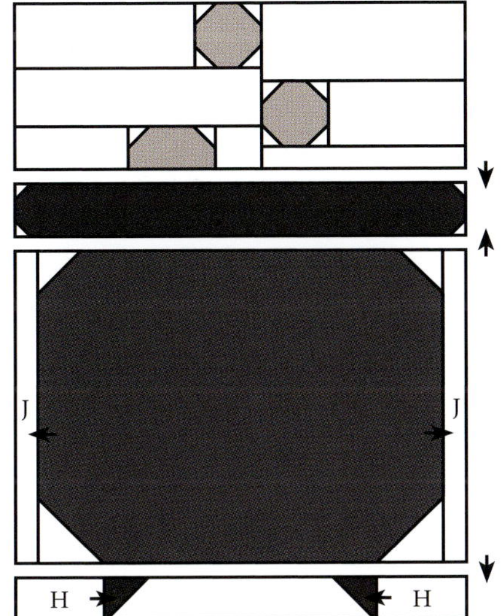
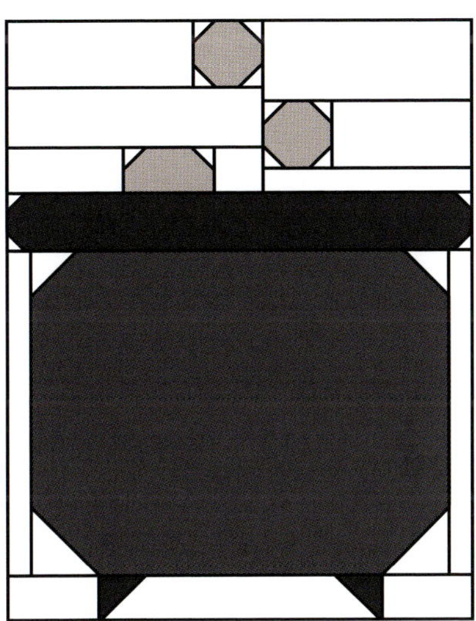

Make one.

Spooky Bat Block

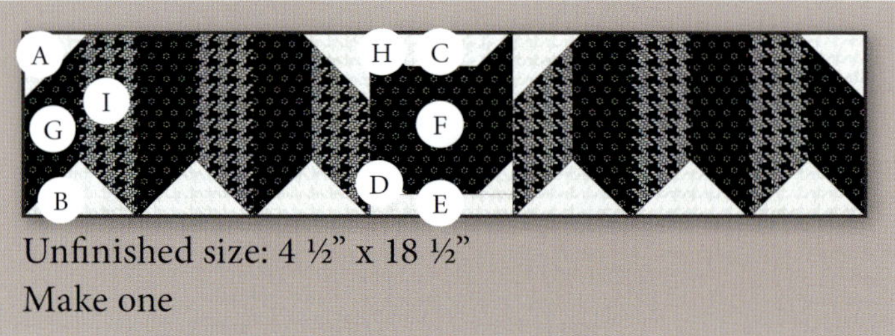

Unfinished size: 4 ½" x 18 ½"
Make one

Cutting Instructions

Background (SKU# 20355-16)

	4 - 2" squares	(A)
	12 - 1 ¾" squares	(B)
	1 - 1 ¼" x 3 ½" rectangle	(C)
	2 - 1 ¼" squares	(D)
	1 - 1" x 3 ½" rectangle	(E)

Bat Head and Wings (SKU# 20354-13)

	1 - 3 ¼" x 3 ½" rectangle	(F)
	6 - 1 ¾" x 4 ½" rectangles	(G)
	2 - 1 ¼" squares	(H)

Bat Wings (SKU# 20355-13)

	6 - 1 ¾" x 4 ½" rectangles	(I)

Piecing Instructions

Draw a diagonal line on the wrong side of the Fabric B squares.

With right sides facing, layer a Fabric B square on the bottom end of a Fabric G rectangle.

Stitch on the drawn line and trim ¼" away from the seam.

Dark Wing Unit should measure 1 ¾" x 4 ½".

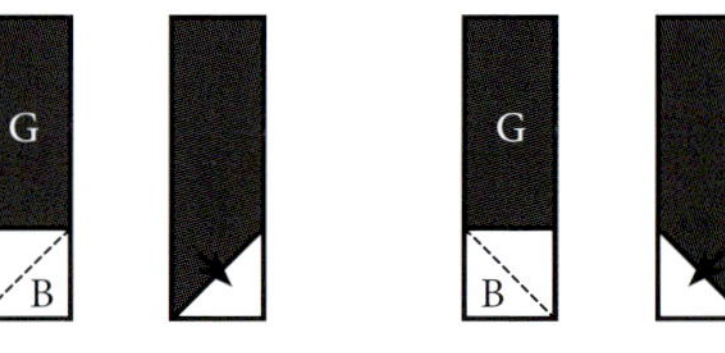

Make three.   Make three.

With right sides facing, layer a Fabric B square on the bottom end of a Fabric I rectangle.

Stitch on the drawn line and trim ¼" away from the seam.

Light Wing Unit should measure 1 ¾" x 4 ½".

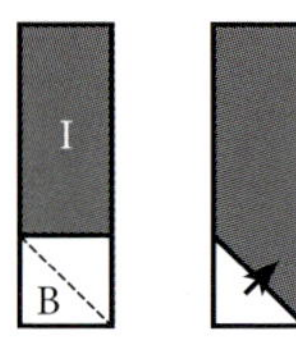

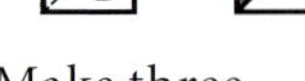

Make three.   Make three.

Assemble Unit.

Partial Left Wing Unit should measure 4 ½" x 8".

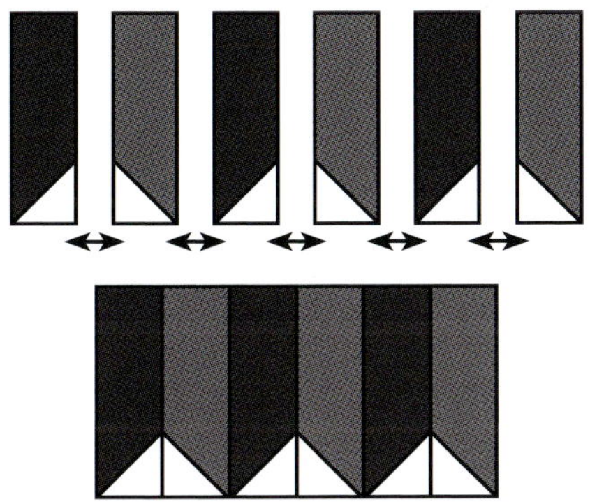

Make one.

Assemble Unit.

Partial Right Wing Unit should measure 4 ½" x 8".

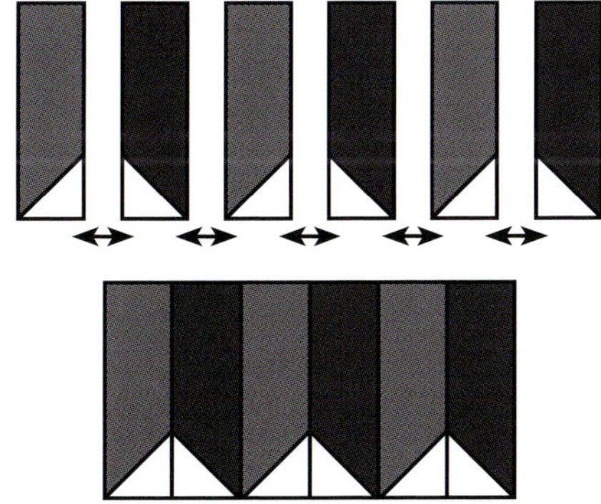

Make one.

Draw a diagonal line on the wrong side of the Fabric A squares.

With right sides facing, layer a Fabric A square on the top left corner of the Partial Left Wing Unit.

Stitch on the drawn line and trim ¼" away from the seam.

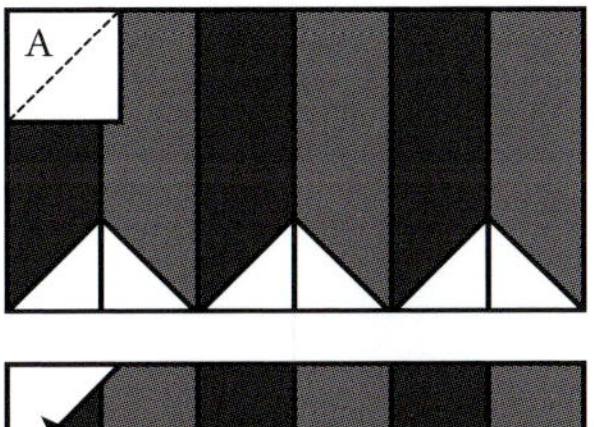

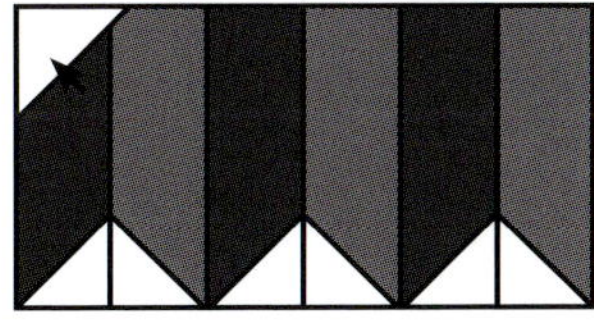

Repeat on the top right corner.

Left Wing Unit should measure 4 ½" x 8".

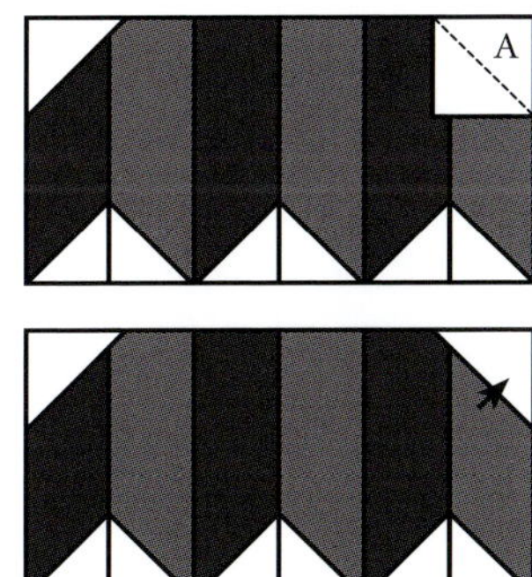

Make one.

Spooky Bat Block

With right sides facing, layer a Fabric A square on the top left corner of the Partial Right Wing Unit.

Stitch on the drawn line and trim ¼" away from the seam.

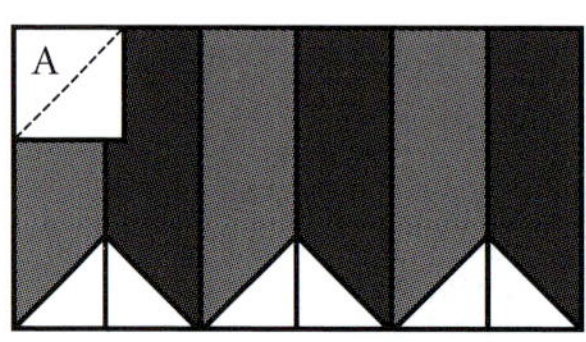

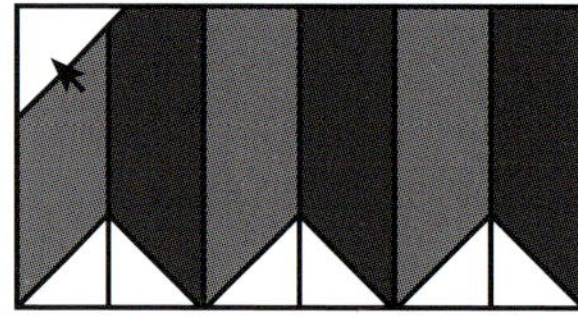

Repeat on the top right corner.

Right Wing Unit should measure 4 ½" x 8".

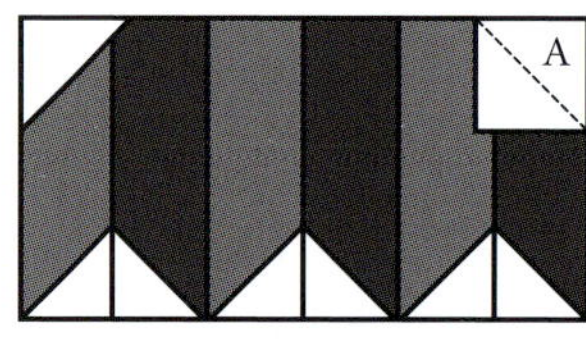

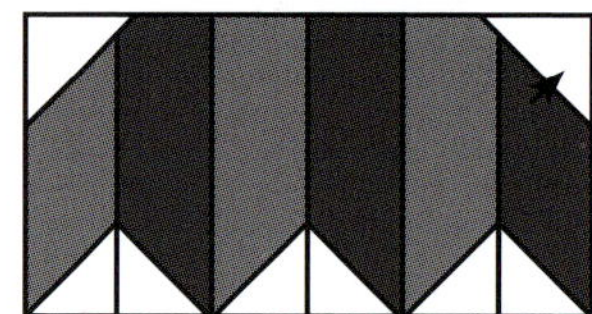

Make one.

Draw a diagonal line on the wrong side of the Fabric H squares.

With right sides facing, layer a Fabric H square on the left end of the Fabric C rectangle.

Stitch on the drawn line and trim ¼" away from the seam.

Repeat on the right end.

Bat Ears Unit should measure 1 ¼" x 3 ½".

Make one.

Draw a diagonal line on the wrong side of the Fabric D squares.

With right sides facing, layer a Fabric D square on the bottom left corner of the Fabric F rectangle.

Stitch on the drawn line and trim ¼" away from the seam.

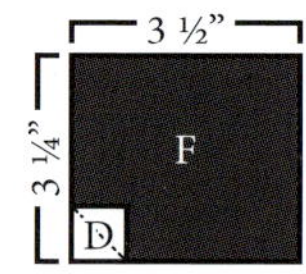

Repeat on the bottom right corner.

Bat Face Unit should measure 3 ¼" x 3 ½".

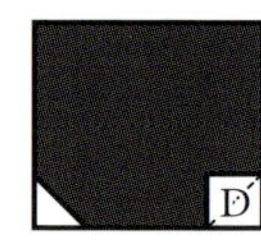

Make one.

 Witch's Night Out by It's Sew Emma

Assemble Block.

Spooky Bat Block should measure 4 ½" x 18 ½".

Make one.

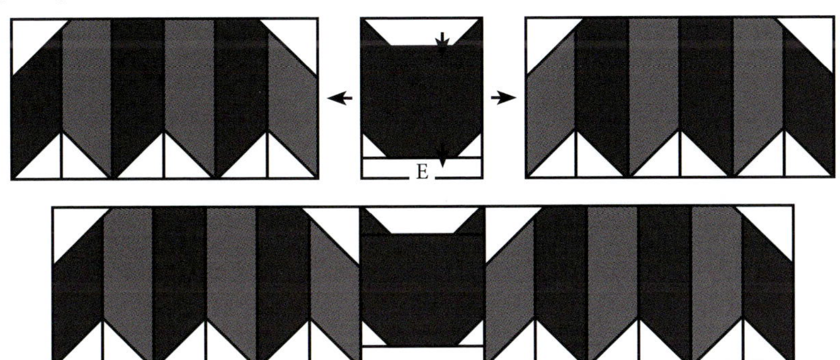

Witch's Hat Block

Unfinished size: 13 ½" x 13 ½"
Make one

Cutting Instructions

Background (SKU# 20355-16)

1 - 5 ½" square	(A)
1 - 3 ½" x 10 ½" rectangle	(B)
1 - 3 ½" x 7 ½" rectangle	(C)
1 - 3 ½" square	(D)
2 - 2 ½" x 3 ½" rectangles	(E)

Witch's Hat (SKU# 20350-13)

1 - 7 ½" square	(F)
1 - 3 ½" square	(G)
1 - 2 ½" x 4 ½" rectangle	(H)
1 - 2 ½" x 3 ½" rectangle	(I)
1 - 1 ½" x 13 ½" rectangle	(J)
1 - 1 ½" x 4 ½" rectangle	(K)
1 - 1 ½" x 2 ½" rectangle	(L)
1 - 1 ½" square	(M)

Hat Buckle (SKU# 20355-11)

2 - 1 ½" x 4 ½" rectangles	(N)
2 - 1 ½" x 2 ½" rectangles	(O)

Hat Ribbon (SKU# 20352-15)

2 - 2 ½" squares	(P)
1 - 1 ½" x 2 ½" rectangle	(Q)

Piecing Instructions

Draw a diagonal line on the wrong side of the Fabric A square.

With right sides facing, layer the Fabric A square on the top left corner of the Fabric F square.

Stitch on the drawn line and trim ¼" away from the seam.

Top Left Witch's Hat Unit should measure 7 ½" x 7 ½".

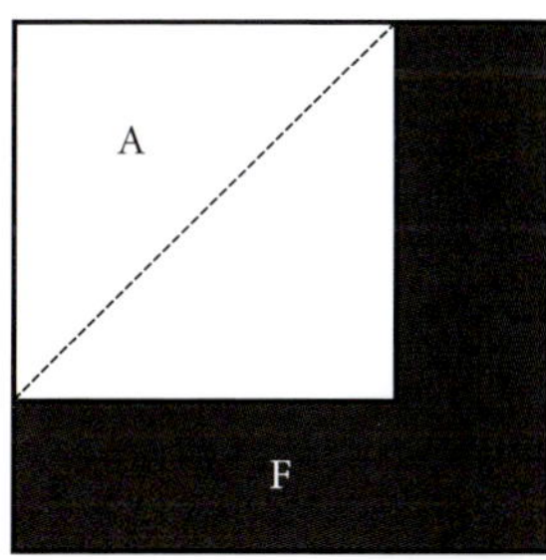

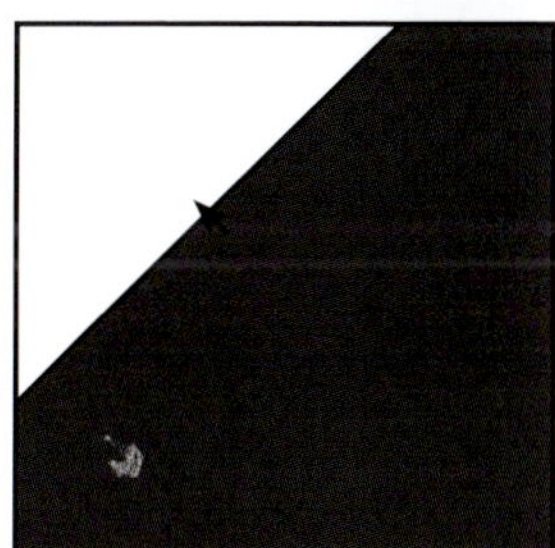

Make one.

Assemble Unit.

Partial Top Witch's Hat Unit should measure 7 ½" x 10 ½".

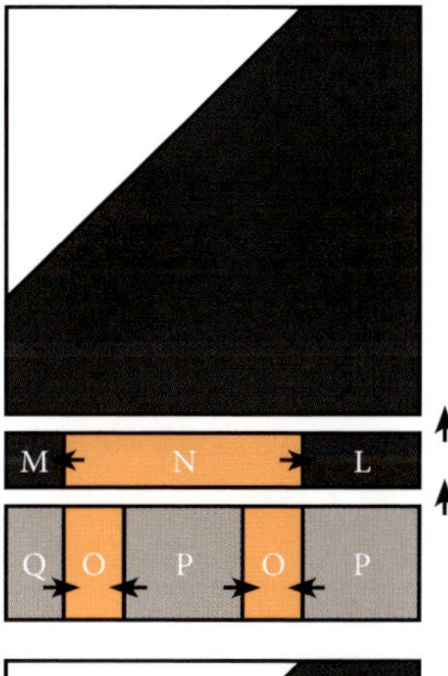

Make one.

Witch's Hat Block

Draw a diagonal line on the wrong side of the Fabric D square.

With right sides facing, layer the Fabric D square with the Fabric G square.

Stitch on the drawn line and trim ¼" away from the seam.

Half Square Triangle Unit should measure 3 ½" x 3 ½".

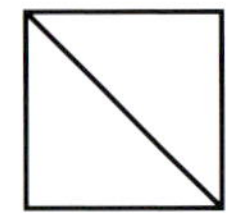  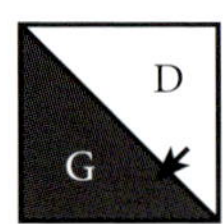

Make one.

Assemble Unit.

Top Witch's Hat Unit should measure 10 ½" x 13 ½".

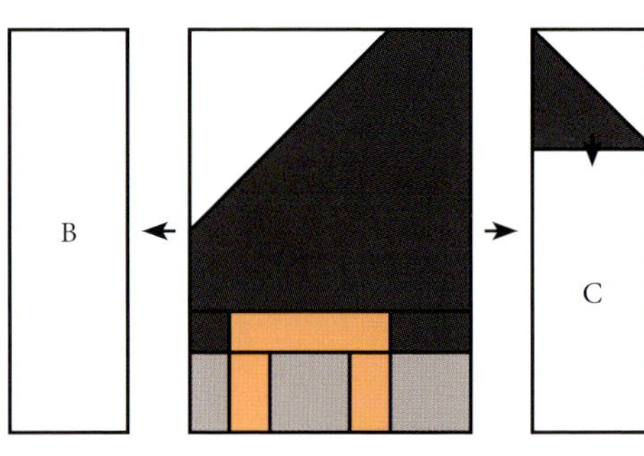

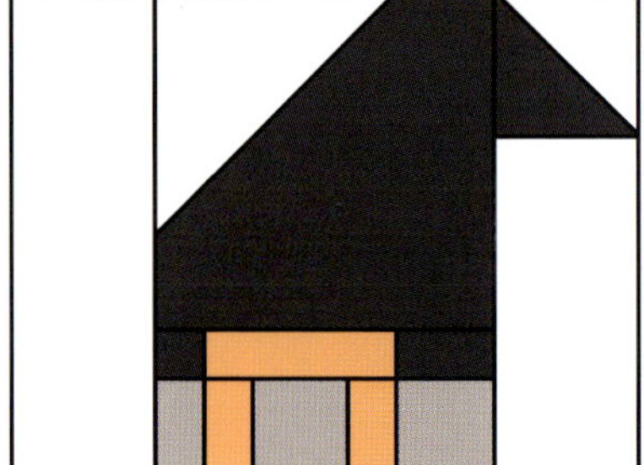

Make one.

Mark a dot 2 ½" down from the top left corner on the wrong side of one Fabric E rectangle.

Draw a line from the top right corner to the dot.

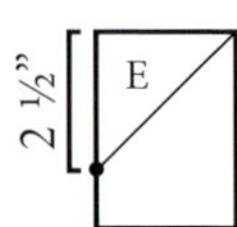

With right sides facing, layer the marked Fabric E rectangle with the Fabric I rectangle.

Stitch on the drawn line and trim ¼" away from the seam.

Left Witch's Hat Brim Unit should measure 2 ½" x 4 ½".

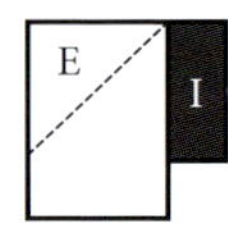  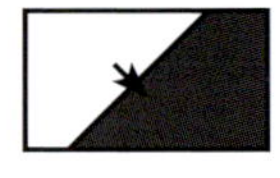

Make one.

Mark a dot 2 ½" down from the top right corner on the wrong side of the remaining Fabric E rectangle.

Draw a line from the top left corner to the dot.

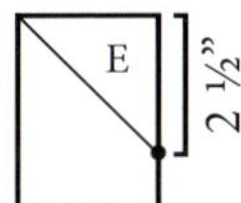

With right sides facing, layer the marked Fabric E rectangle with the Fabric H rectangle.

Stitch on the drawn line and trim ¼" away from the seam.

Right Witch's Hat Brim Unit should measure 2 ½" x 5 ½".

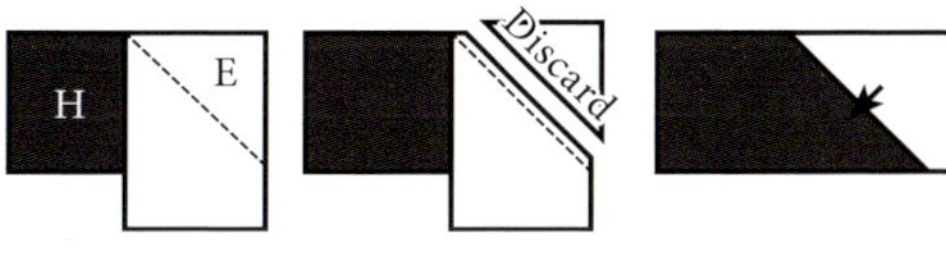

Make one.

Assemble Unit.

Witch's Hat Brim Unit should measure 2 ½" x 13 ½".

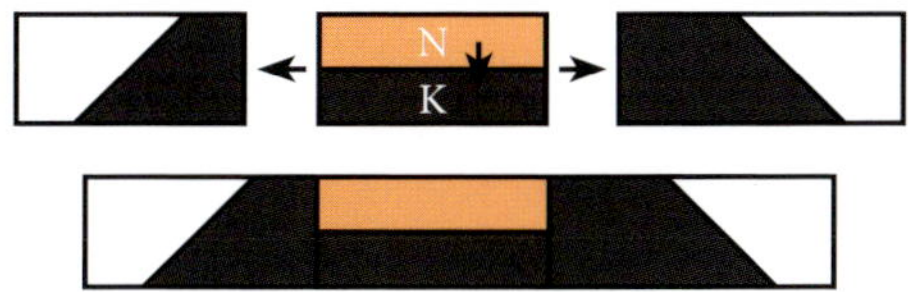

Make one.

Assemble Block.

Witch's Hat Block should measure 13 ½" x 13 ½".

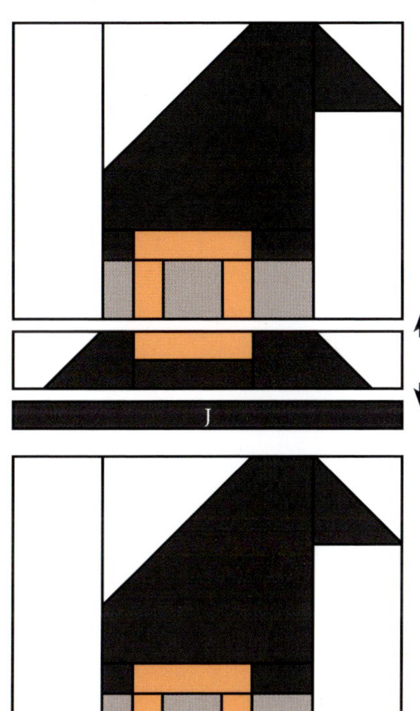

Make one.

57 ½" x 64 ½"

Cutting Instructions

Background (SKU# 20355-16)

	3 - 6" x 9 ½" rectangles	(A)
	1 - 5 ½" x 8 ½" rectangle	(B)
	7 - 3 ½" x WOF strips	(C)
	1 - 3 ½" x 5 ½" rectangle	(D)
	2 - 3" x 8" rectangles	(E)
	5 - 2 ½" x WOF strips	(F)
	2 - 2 ½" x 18 ½" rectangles	(G)
	2 - 2 ½" x 13 ½" rectangles	(H)
	1 - 2 ½" x 8" rectangle	(I)
	4 - 2 ¼" x 13 ½" rectangles	(J)
	2 - 2" x 13 ½" rectangles	(K)
	5 - 2" x 5 ½" rectangles	(L)
	6 - 1 ¾" x 5 ½" rectangles	(M)
	3 - 1 ½" 13 ½" rectangles	(N)
	1 - 1 ½" x 5 ½" rectangle	(O)
	1 - 1" x 20 ½" strip	(P)
	1 - 1" x 14 ½" rectangle	(Q)
	1 - 1" x 9 ½" rectangle	(R)

Binding (SKU# 20355-13)

	7 - 2 ½" x WOF strips	(S)

Quilt Rows

Assemble Unit using the following blocks:

- Flying Geese Pumpkin Block
- Striped Pumpkin Block
- Chevron Pumpkin Block
- Triangular Pumpkin Block
- Starlight Pumpkin Block

First Row Unit should measure 13 ½" x 20 ½".

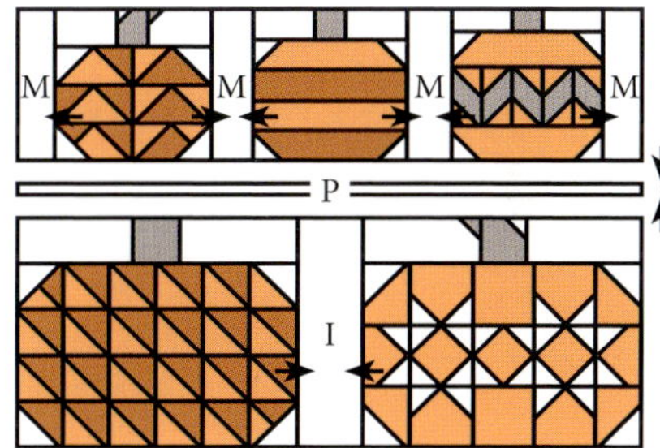

Make one.

Witch's Night Out
Finishing

Assemble Row using the following blocks:
- Chevron Pumpkin Block
- Striped Pumpkin Block
- Witch's Hat Block
- First Row Unit
- Mosaic Pumpkin Block

First Row should measure 13 ½" x 51 ½".

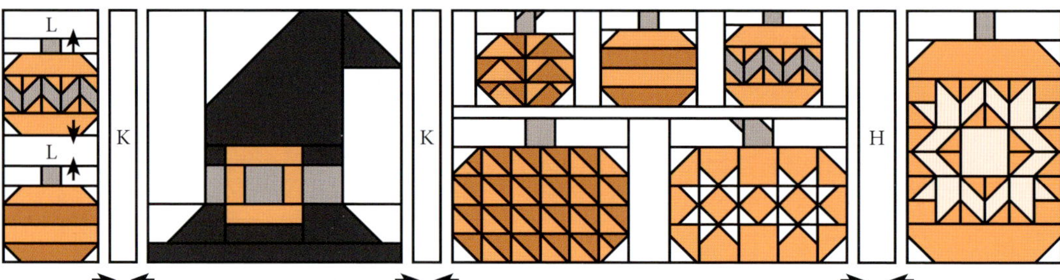

Make one.

Assemble Row using the following blocks:
- Triangular Pumpkin Block
- Chained Pumpkin Block
- Flying Geese Pumpkin Block
- Black Cat and Broomstick Block

Second Row should measure 13 ½" x 51 ½".

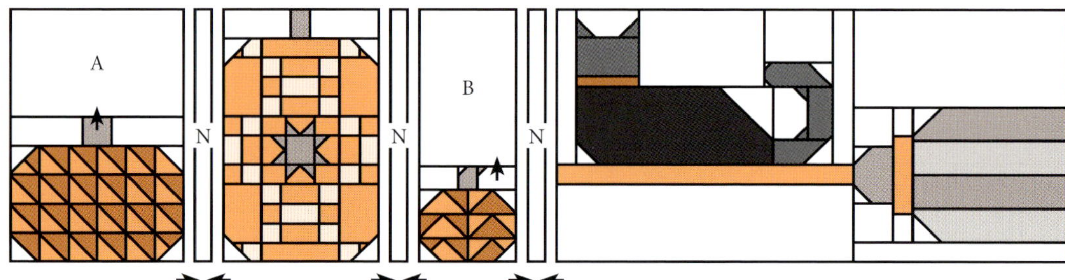

Make one.

Assemble Unit using the following blocks:

- Spooky Bat Block
- Flying Geese Pumpkin Block
- Striped Pumpkin Block
- Chevron Pumpkin Block

Bat and Pumpkins Third Row Unit should measure 13 ½" x 18 ½".

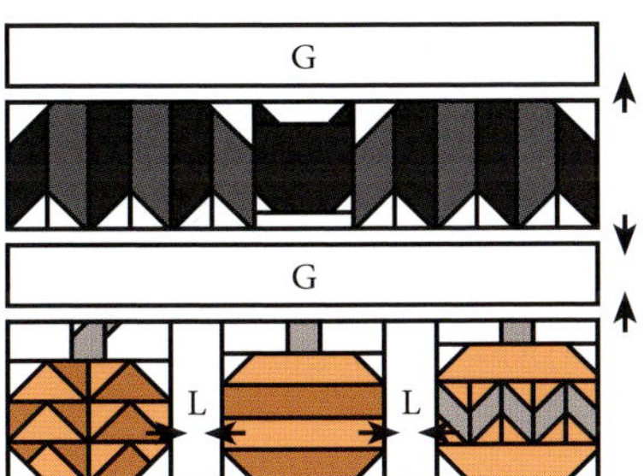

Make one.

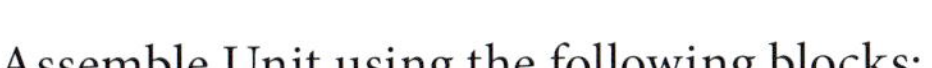

Assemble Unit using the following blocks:

- Striped Pumpkin Block
- Chevron Pumpkin Block
- Starlight Pumpkin Block

Left Pumpkins Third Row Unit should measure 13 ½" x 14 ½".

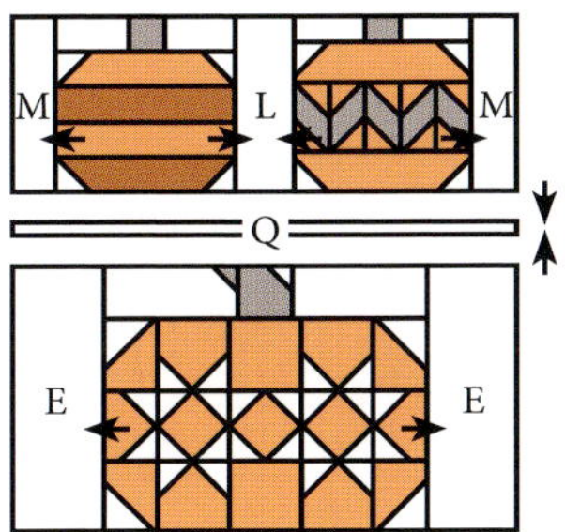

Make one.

Assemble Unit using the following blocks:

- Flying Geese Pumpkin Block
- Triangular Pumpkin Block

Right Pumpkins Third Row Unit should measure 9 ½" x 13 ½".

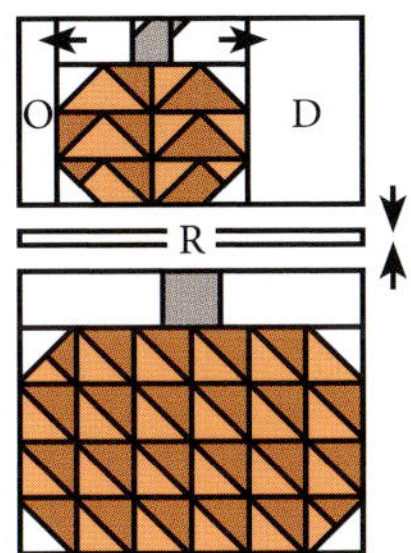

Make one.

Assemble Unit using the following blocks:
- Bat and Pumpkin Third Row Unit
- Left Pumpkins Third Row Unit
- Mosaic Pumpkin Block
- Right Pumpkins Third Row Unit

Third Row should measure 13 ½" x 51 ½".

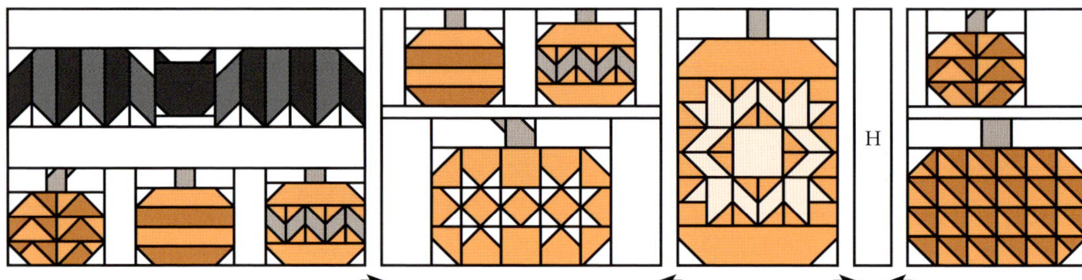

Make one.

Assemble Row using the following blocks:
- Mosaic Pumpkin Block
- Triangular Pumpkin Block
- Bubbling Cauldron Block
- Starlight Pumpkin Block
- Chained Pumpkin Block

Fourth Row should measure 13 ½" x 51 ½".

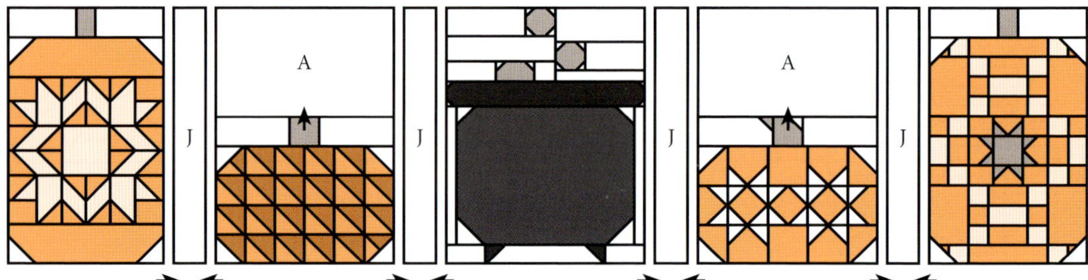

Make one.

Quilt Center

Piece the Fabric F strips end to end.

Subcut into:

      3 - 2 ½" x 51 ½" strips (Sashing - F)

Assemble Quilt Center.

Quilt Center should measure 51 ½" x 58 ½".

Borders

Piece the Fabric C strips end to end.

Subcut into:

       2 - 3 ½" x 58 ½" strips (Side Borders - C1)

       2 - 3 ½" x 57 ½" strips (Top and Bottom Borders - C2)

Attach the Side Borders.

Attach the Top and Bottom Borders.

Finishing

Piece the Fabric S strips end to end for binding.

Quilt and bind as desired.

Witch's Night Out Finishing

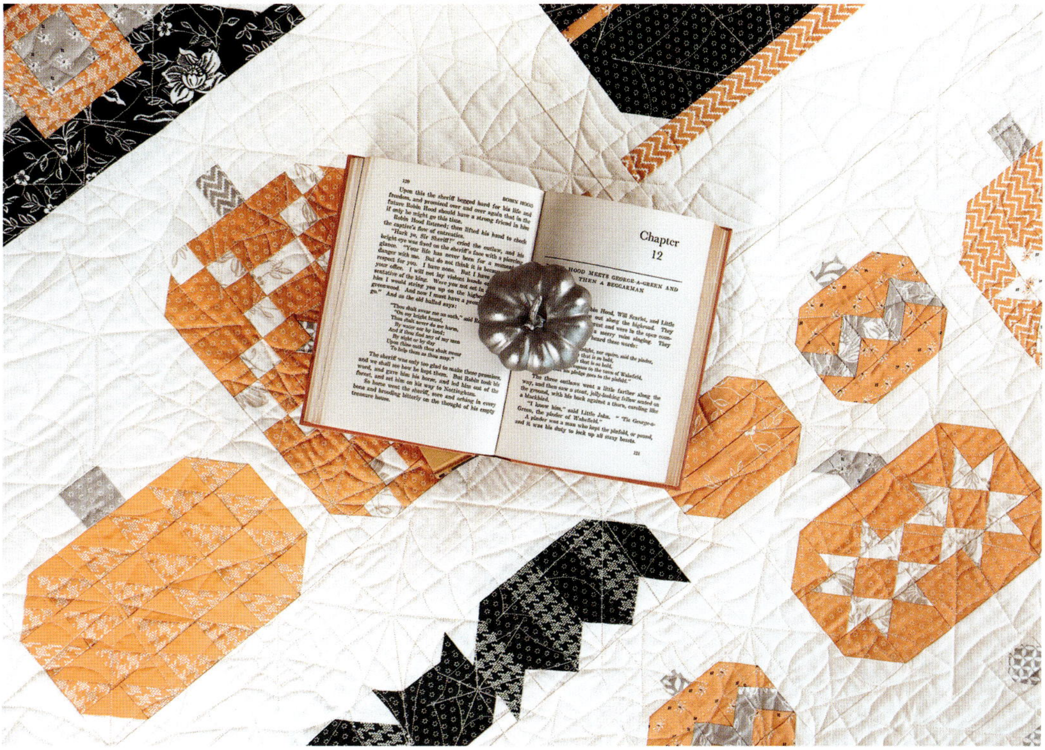

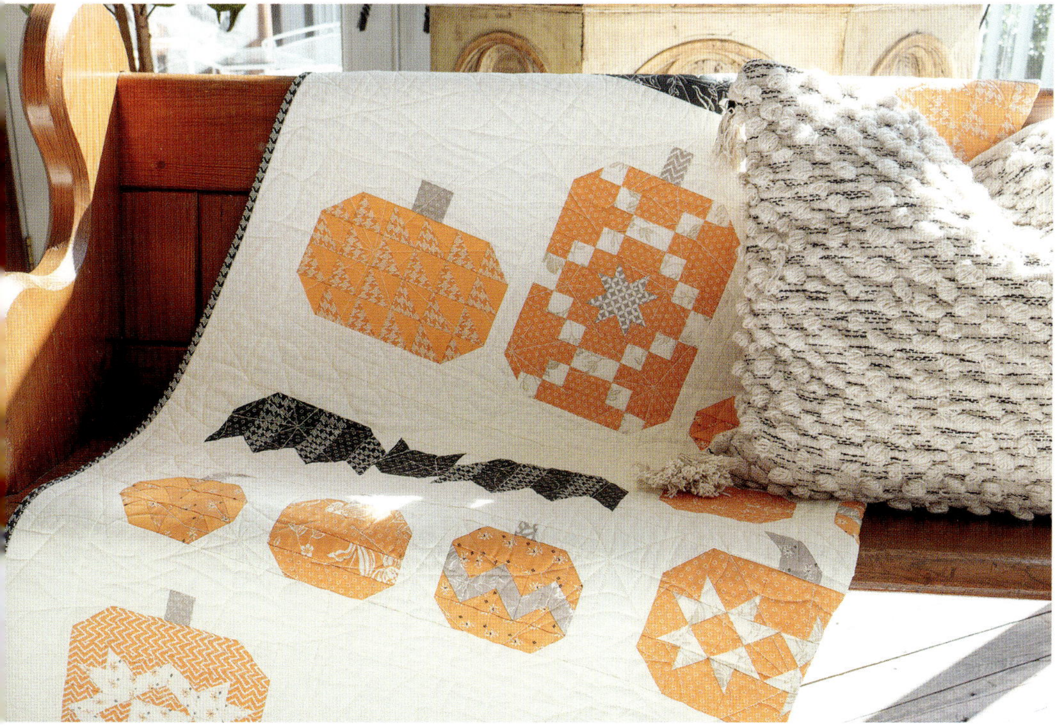

Pumpkin Patch Tablerunner

16 ½" x 58 ½"

Fabric Requirements

20350-11
Blocks
10" square

20350-15
Blocks
Fat Eighth

20350-26
Blocks
Fat Quarter

20351-15
Blocks
10" square

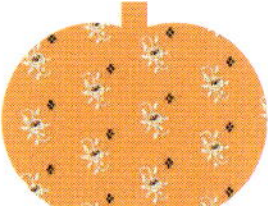

20352-11
Blocks
Fat Quarter

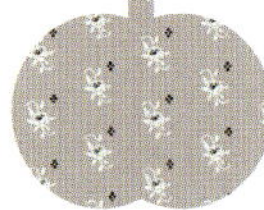

20352-15
Blocks
10" square

20352-16
Blocks
Fat Eighth

20353-11
Blocks
Fat Quarter

20353-15
Blocks
10" square

20354-11
Blocks
Fat Quarter

20354-15
Blocks
10" square

20355-11
Blocks
Fat Eighth

20355-16
Background
1 ⅛ yards

20356-11
Binding
½ yard

20356-15
Blocks
10" square

9900-162
Blocks
Fat Quarter

20352-16
Backing
2 yards

Pumpkin Patch Tablerunner

Refer to pages 4 to 5 for block instructions.

Chevron Pumpkin Block

Background (SKU# 20355-16)		
	8 - 1 ½" squares	(A)
	4 - 1 ¼" x 2 ½" rectangles	(B)
Print Pumpkin (SKU# 20352-11)		
	4 - 1 ⅝" x 5 ½" rectangles	(C)
	20 - 1 ½" squares	(D)
Chevron (SKU# 20350-15)		
	10 - 1 ½" x 2 ½" rectangles	(E)
Pumpkin Stem (SKU# 20351-15)		
	2 - 1 ¼" x 1 ½" rectangles	(F)

Chevron Pumpkin Block should measure 5 ½" x 5 ½".

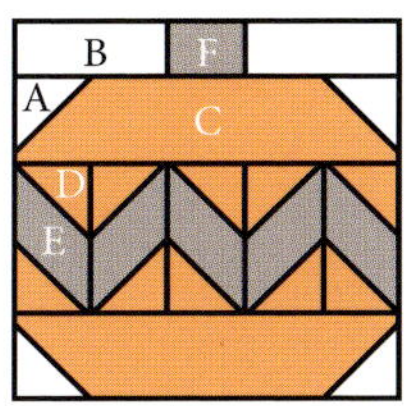

Make two.

Refer to pages 6 to 8 for block instructions.

Flying Geese Pumpkin Block

Background (SKU# 20355-16)		
	4 - 1 ¾" x 2 ½" rectangles	(A)
	8 - 1 ¾" squares	(B)
	2 - 1" squares	(C)
Solid Pumpkin (SKU# 9900-162)		
	6 - 1 ¾" x 3" rectangles	(D)
	10 - 1 ¾" squares	(E)
Print Pumpkin (SKU# 20352-11)		
	6 - 1 ¾" x 3" rectangles	(F)
	10 - 1 ¾" squares	(G)
Pumpkin Stem (SKU# 20350-15)		
	2 - 1 ½" x 1 ¾" rectangles	(H)
	2 - 1" squares	(I)

Flying Geese Pumpkin Block should measure 5 ½" x 5 ½".

Make two.

Pumpkin Patch Tablerunner

Refer to pages 10 to 11 for block instructions.

Striped Pumpkin Block

Background (SKU# 20355-16)

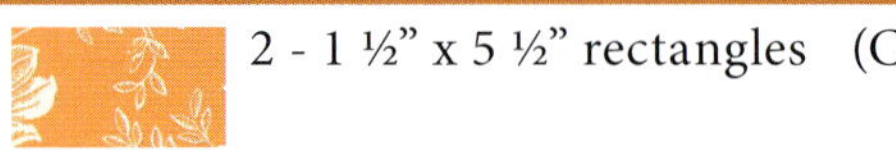

2 - 1 ½" x 2 ½" rectangles	(A)
4 - 1 ½" squares	(B)

Print Pumpkin One (SKU# 20350-11)

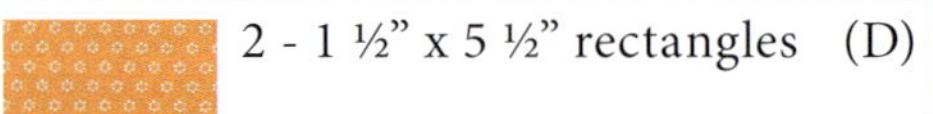

2 - 1 ½" x 5 ½" rectangles	(C)

Print Pumpkin Two (SKU# 20354-11)

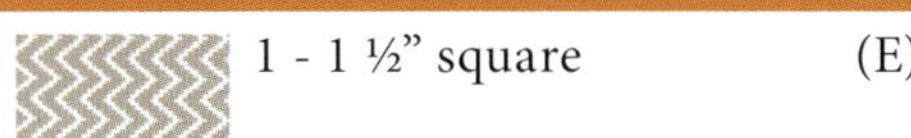

2 - 1 ½" x 5 ½" rectangles	(D)

Pumpkin Stem (SKU# 20353-15)

1 - 1 ½" square	(E)

Striped Pumpkin Block should measure 5 ½" x 5 ½".

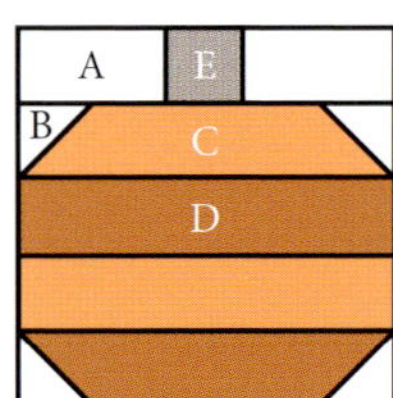

Make one.

Refer to pages 12 to 15 for block instructions.

Starlight Pumpkin Block

Background (SKU# 20355-16)

2 - 2" x 4 ¼" rectangles	(A)
4 - 2" squares	(B)
1 - 1 ½" square	(C)

Pumpkin (SKU# 20354-11)

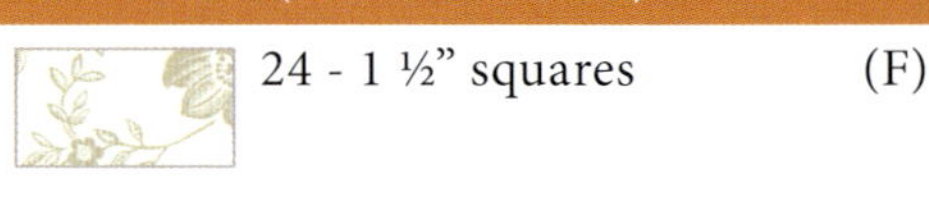

9 - 2 ½" squares	(D)
6 - 2" x 2 ½" rectangles	(E)

Star Points (SKU# 20350-26)

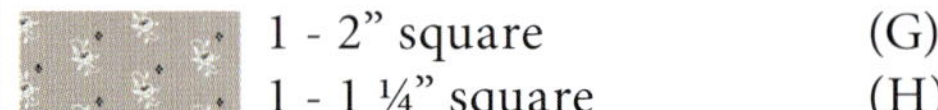

24 - 1 ½" squares	(F)

Pumpkin Stem (SKU# 20352-15)

1 - 2" square	(G)
1 - 1 ¼" square	(H)

Starlight Pumpkin Block should measure 8" x 9 ½".

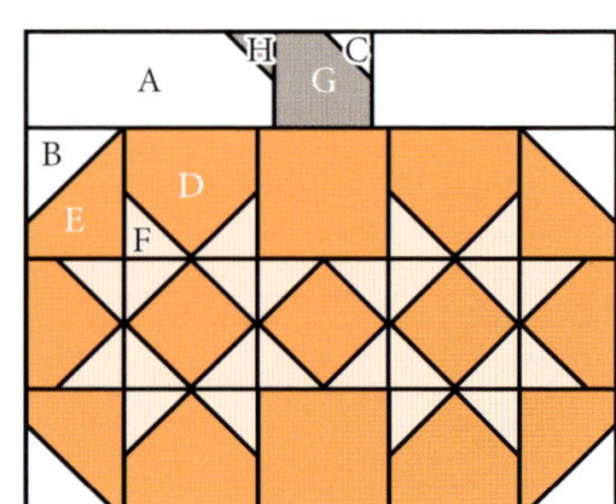

Make one.

Refer to pages 16 to 17 for block instructions.

Triangular Pumpkin Block

Background (SKU# 20355-16)

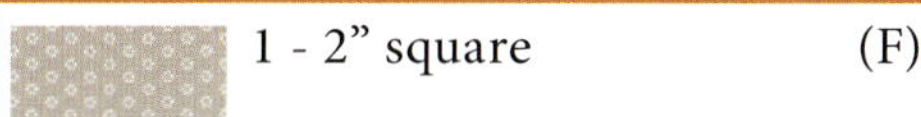

2 - 2" x 4 ¼" rectangles	(A)
2 - 2 ⅜" squares	(B)
2 - 2" squares	(C)

Print Pumpkin (SKU# 20355-11)

12 - 2 ⅜" squares	(D)

Solid Pumpkin (SKU# 9900-162)

12 - 2 ⅜" squares	(E)

Pumpkin Stem (SKU# 20354-15)

1 - 2" square	(F)

Triangular Pumpkin Block should measure 8" x 9 ½".

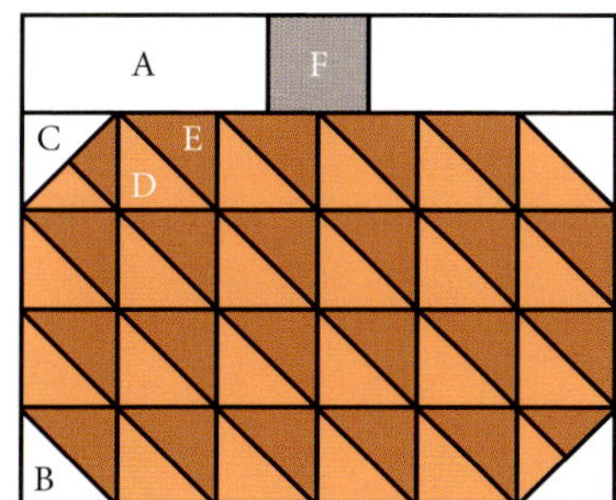

Make one.

Refer to pages 18 to 21 for block instructions.

Chained Pumpkin Block

Background (SKU# 20355-16)

2 - 2" x 4" rectangles	(A)
4 - 2" squares	(B)

Pumpkin (SKU# 20354-11)

4 - 2 ½" x 3 ½" rectangles	(C)
2 - 1 ¾" x 2" rectangles	(D)
2 - 1 ½" x 4 ½" rectangles	(E)
4 - 1 ½" x 2 ½" rectangles	(F)
4 - 1 ½" x 2" rectangles	(G)
4 - 1 ½" x 1 ¾" rectangles	(H)
12 - 1 ½" squares	(I)

Chains (SKU# 20350-26)

2 - 1 ½" x 2 ½" rectangles	(J)
2 - 1 ½" x 2" rectangles	(K)
16 - 1 ½" squares	(L)

Star (SKU# 20356-15)

1 - 2" square	(M)
8 - 1 ¼" squares	(N)

Pumpkin Stem (SKU# 20353-15)

1 - 1 ½" x 2" rectangle	(O)

Chained Pumpkin Block should measure 8 ½" x 13 ½".

Make one.

Pumpkin Patch Tablerunner

Refer to pages 22 to 25 for block instructions.

Mosaic Pumpkin Block

Background (SKU# 20355-16)

2 - 2" x 4" rectangles	(A)
4 - 2" squares	(B)

Pumpkin (SKU# 20353-11)

2 - 2 ½" x 8 ½" rectangles	(C)
12 - 1 ¾" x 2" rectangles	(D)
16 - 1 ¾" squares	(E)

Mosaic (SKU# 20352-16)

1 - 3" square	(F)
12 - 1 ¾" x 3" rectangles	(G)
4 - 1 ¾" squares	(H)

Pumpkin Stem (SKU# 20354-15)

1 - 1 ½" x 2" rectangle	(I)

Tablerunner Finishing

Background (SKU# 20355-16)

1 - 6" x 9 ½" rectangle	(A)
2 - 5 ½" x 8 ½" rectangles	(B)
1 - 4 ½" x 5 ½" rectangle	(C)
2 - 2" x 5 ½" rectangles	(D)
6 - 1 ½" x 13 ½" rectangles	(E)
1 - 1" x 9 ½" rectangle	(F)
2 - 2" x 16 ½" rectangles	(G)
3 - 2" x WOF strips	(H)

Binding (SKU# 20356-11)

5 - 2 ½" x WOF strips	(I)

Mosaic Pumpkin Block should measure 8 ½" x 13 ½".

Make one.

Tablerunner Center

Assemble Unit using the following blocks:

- Chevron Pumpkin Block
- Triangular Pumpkin Block

Pumpkin Patch Unit should measure 9 ½" x 13 ½".

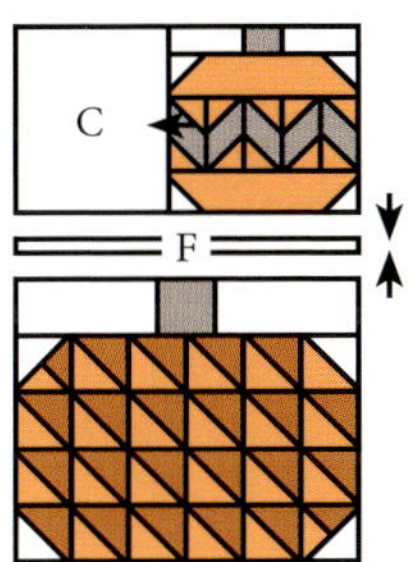
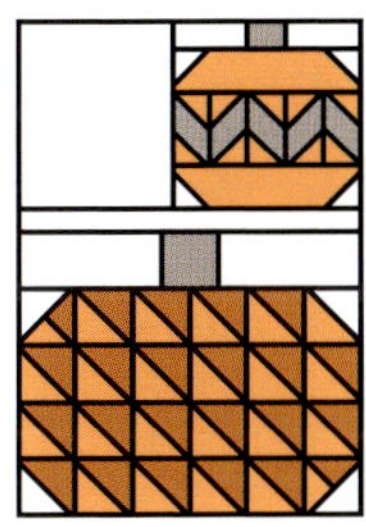

Make one.

Assemble Tablerunner Center.

Tablerunner Center should measure 13 ½" x 55 ½".

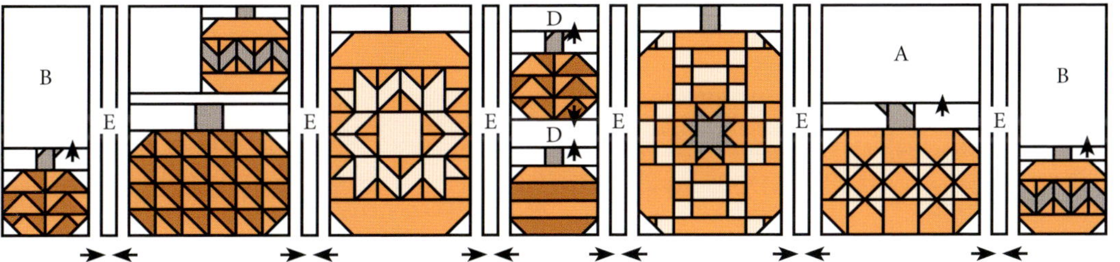

Pumpkin Patch Tablerunner

Borders

Piece the Fabric H strips end to end.

Subcut into:

2 - 2" x 55 ½" strips (Top and Bottom Borders - H)

Attach the Top and Bottom Borders.

Attach the side borders using the Fabric G rectangles.

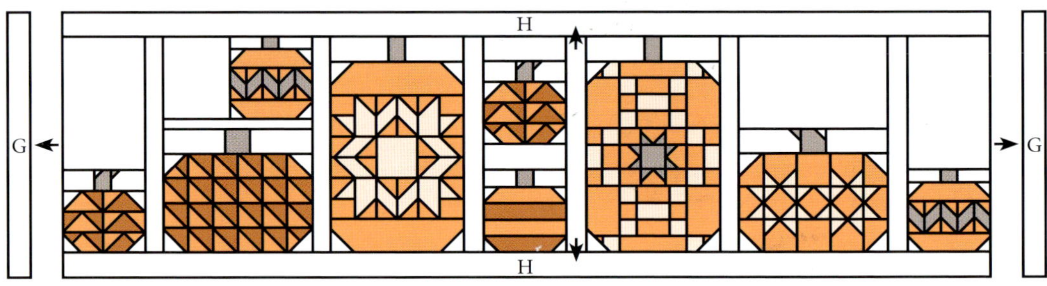

Finishing

Piece the Fabric I strips end to end for binding.

Quilt and bind as desired.